Award in Education

Understanding and Using Inclusive Teaching and Learning Approaches in Education and Training

Nabeel Zaidi

LLB (Hons), LLM, Pg.Dip. DMS, MBA, Cert. Ed., Barrister

About this book

Understanding and Using Inclusive Teaching and Learning Approaches in Education and Training is the second book in the *Award in Education and Training* series and covers each aspect of the Award in Education and Training unit of the same name. Like the first book on *Understanding Roles, Responsibilities and Relationships in Education and Training*, this book is mapped directly to each of the learning outcomes and assessment criteria for the unit across all awarding organisations. It provides detailed practical explanation and links to various other resources so that whether you are new to teaching or already in a teaching or related role, there will be a detailed examination of inclusive teaching and learning approaches in education and training. People purchasing this book may find it useful to have a copy of the first book in the series (*Understanding Roles, Responsibilities and Relationships in Education and Training*) as background.

About the author

The author has been in the further education sector since 1996, occupying various lecturing, middle and senior management and consultancy roles, including working with several awarding organisations, undertaking quality assurance assignments, delivering professional training to the education sector on equality and diversity and the Ofsted common inspection framework and developing and delivering on undergraduate and post-graduate business management programmes and teaching qualifications. He is also a Reviewer for the Quality Assurance Agency (QAA) and runs his own college and consultancy company.

Nabeel holds various academic and professional qualifications and titles, including being a qualified Barrister, an MBA in Educational Management (University of Leicester), a Certificate in Education (Institute of Education), a Post-Graduate Diploma in Professional Legal Skills (Inns of Court School of Law / City University), a Master's degree in Law (University College London), a degree in Law (Queen Mary's College, University of London), and a Post-Graduate Diploma in Management Studies.

Contents

3

Ways to create an inclusive teaching and learning environment 73

Introduction

Understanding and Using Inclusive Teaching and Learning Approaches in Education and Training is an optional unit of the Award in Education and Training across all awarding organisations. It also includes the underpinning principles for the micro-teach element. The purpose of this textbook is to provide candidates studying the *Award in Education and Training* with robust underpinning subject content and guidance to meet the assessment criteria of the unit and provide opportunities for further research and investigation.

Definition of roles for the purposes of this textbook:

Role	Definition
Lecturer/Teacher/ Trainer/Tutor/Assessor	the person taking the Award in Education and Training qualification.
Learner/Student	the person being taught or assessed by the Lecturer/ Teacher/Trainer/Tutor/Assessor.
AET Tutor	the person delivering/facilitating the Award in Education and Training qualification.

Inclusive teaching and learning approaches in education and training

1. Features of inclusive teaching and learning

(a) Definition

Inclusive learning seeks to ensure that all learners have sufficient opportunity to be included and actively involved in the learning process and that they are treated fairly, equally and their differences are recognised, accommodated and where relevant celebrated. These aspects are considered below.

(b) Equality of opportunity

Within the further education, learning and skills sector, equality of opportunity is interpreted to mean that everyone has the opportunity to acquire relevant skills, competencies and qualifications to compete. It expects learning providers to have plans[1], policies[2], procedures[3] and practices[4] in place that prevent discrimination on any of the nine protected characteristics under the Equality Act 2010. These include the following:

- Age
- Disability
- Gender reassignment
- Marriage and civil partnership
- Pregnancy and maternity
- Race
- Religion or belief
- Sex
- Sexual orientation

---

[1] These are normally strategic in nature, such as a learning provider's strategic plan.
[2] These are statements of intent (i.e. what the learning provider intends to do and how).
[3] These are to do with implementation of policies.
[4] This is the 'reality on the ground' (i.e. what the learning provider and its staff actually do).

In the case of 'disability' and 'pregnancy and maternity' learning providers can provide favourable treatment[5] or special treatment[6] respectively. That is, taking steps to make reasonable adjustments that minimise the disadvantage faced by learners with disabilities or as a result of pregnancy and maternity. This includes, but is not limited to, physical adjustments to the premises, learning resources, assessment methods and course duration and delivery methods. For example, a learner who is diagnosed as blind is likely to be allowed 100% extra time in an examination and allocated a reader and scribe to read questions and note and read back the responses for them.

The interpretation of equality of opportunity has been extended further by Ofsted, an inspection body that normally regulates funded learning provision from Entry Level 1 to Level 3.[7] Learning providers that are inspected by Oftsed are expected to prevent discrimination against and promote equality for the following groups of learner:

- disabled learners
- learners with special needs
- boys/men
- girls/women
- groups of learners whose prior attainment may be different from that of other groups
- those who are academically more or less able
- learners for whom English is an additional language
- minority ethnic learners
- Gypsy, Roma and Traveller learners
- learners qualifying for a bursary scheme award

---

[5] "... disabled people can be treated more favourably than non-disabled people, but one disabled person cannot be treated more favourably than another disabled person." Paragraph 54 of *The First Report on the UN Convention*, November 2011.

[6] "An employer does not discriminate against a man where it affords a woman 'special treatment' in connection with childbirth and pregnancy.", Paragraph 8.43, *Employment Statutory Code of Practice*, Equality and Human Rights Commission, January 2011

[7] Level 3 is equivalent to AS / A level and BTEC Nationals.

- looked after children
- lesbian, gay and bisexual learners
- transgender learners
- young carers
- learners from low-income backgrounds
- older learners
- learners of different religions and beliefs
- ex-offenders
- women returners
- teenage mothers
- other vulnerable groups.

Awarding organisations and accreditation, inspection and review bodies expect learning providers to have equality and diversity policies and procedures in place.

(c) Diversity

While the concept of diversity has no legal definition and therefore is not legally regulated, it can be viewed as 'recognising difference'. This can include recognising and celebrating differences in race, culture, belief, nationality, sexual orientation and so on. The application of and commitment to diversity depends to a large extent on the senior management team of a learning provider and their expectations of the organisation in relation to diversity.

A good example of diversity can be seen in the higher education sector, where some universities have introduced the concept of *internationalising the curriculum*.[8] This includes the study of a

---

[8] "Internationalising the curriculum involves providing students with global perspectives of their discipline and giving them a broader knowledge base for their future careers. [Institutions] can also help to provide them with a set of values and skills to operate in diverse cultural environments; skills often labelled 'intercultural competencies' or 'cross-cultural capabilities'.", p3, *Internationalising the Curriculum*, The Higher Education Academy, 2014

subject area and considers its application in other countries, providing global perspectives of their subject, so that learners are not limited to research and examples from the UK, Europe and USA, but can also consider those from other countries, for instance, the practice of fast food in India and Pakistan: fast food providers, such as McDonalds have had to adjust their meat menu in India and Pakistan to meet religious requirements. This is important in developing an understanding of cultural, religious and other differences and has implications for developing 'intercultural competencies'.[9]

Taking this a step further, learning providers can consider the pedagogical[10] and andragogical[11] differences of its learners from different educational, cultural or domicile backgrounds and provide support mechanisms to accommodate those differences. For instance, an adult learner whose previous experience of education in the UK or abroad has been of preparing for examinations, may need support sessions in place to adjust to a course that requires written assignments and presentations. Putting such sessions and training in place not only recognises difference, but also promotes inclusivity at curriculum level and should in turn improve learner performance in written assignments and presentations.

Case studies and learning resources may include the study of organisations from a wide range of countries, including those

---

[9] "The development of intercultural competence is a dynamic, ongoing, interactive self-reflective learning process that transforms attitudes, skills and knowledge for effective communication and interaction across cultures and contexts.", Freeman, M (2009), *Embedding the Development of Intercultural Competence in Business Higher Education*

[10] These are the methods and practices in teaching, especially of children (up to the age of 18), where the focus is on the teacher's methods of transferring knowledge to a learner, who is dependent on the teacher's methods and understanding. The teacher controls the learning experience for children, and most teaching is based on a rigid curricula. A great deal of importance is placed on the grades achieved.

[11] These are the methods and practices used in teaching adults, focusing on independent, self-directed and/or cooperative learning, where adults exercise control over much of their learning experience, with grades being less important to them than gaining knowledge and skills.

familiar to the learners. Alternatively, assignments and case studies could permit learners to choose their own organisations or areas for research. Recognising and accommodating difference and providing choice can be viewed as an aspect of diversity and a means of promoting learner engagement and motivation.[12]

(d) Active engagement, motivation and differentiation

Understanding learner aspirations, expectations and what learners hope to achieve from completing the course should inform teaching, learning and assessment strategies and the content of the learning resources and examples or case studies used. For instance, the case studies and examples used to demonstrate concepts for 16-18 year-old Business learners is likely to be different from those used for current managers aged 30+ studying on a Business programme.

With the 16-18 year-old learners, they will have less work-related experience than the group of managers aged 30+ and so the case studies and examples need to build concepts more gradually, especially when considering management and human resources issues, whereas for experienced managers on a Business programme, examples can draw on learners' own experiences. The ability to distinguish and respond to the different learning needs, abilities and past experiences of learners is an important element of differentiation[13] and underpins active engagement and motivation.

---

[12] For a more detailed treatment of equality and diversity read: *Equality and Diversity: Embedding Equality and Diversity into the Curriculum - a literature review* (available from Amazon, CreateSpace and HopeBookStore) and *Equality and Diversity: Embedding Equality and Diversity into a Postgraduate Management Programme for International Students - a case study* (available from Amazon, CreateSpace and HopeBookStore).

[13] This can be viewed as the process by which differences between learners are accommodated so that all students in a group have the best possible chance of learning. It can be divided into 7 categories, including

An effective differentiated session would include lesson plans that have learning resources, activities, teaching, learning and assessment strategies that cater for different learner needs and abilities. In a class of 16-18 year-olds studying A level Physics for example, work experience may be less varied than for a class of adult learners, but the range of academic backgrounds and current ability range may be more varied. A good session for the adult learners would, where relevant, draw upon learners' past experiences and background and ask them to share such experiences so as to provide real life insight into the topic being discussed (e.g. an HR Manager discussing their application of equality and diversity in their workplace recently). Such contributions are likely to keep learners engaged, recognise the relevance of their past experience to their current studies and thereby increase their confidence and motivation for the course.

Meanwhile, for the class of 16-18 year-olds studying A level Physics, there may well be learners with varying levels of aptitude for the subject, with those on target to achieve a grade D/E, or a C/D or an A/B in the subject. The lecturer will need to have strategies planned for each of these ability ranges that provide support for those who are struggling with new concepts, re-enforce learning for those that are coping with the new concepts and provide academic stretch

---

differentiation by **task** (different tasks or exercises for different ability ranges), by **grouping** (mixed-ability groups), by **resources** (varying resources according to learner needs and abilities, such as providing basic resources and complex/advanced resources), by **pace** (learners working at a different pace can be given support or more challenging activities, so that whether a learner is falling behind, keeping up or completing exercises early in a session, support and extension materials ensure that all learners maintain momentum), by **outcome** (all students undertake the same task, but a range of results / grades are expected and considered as acceptable), by **dialogue and support** (identifying which learners need detailed explanations in simple language and which learners can engage in dialogue at a more sophisticated level. The teacher may also use directed questioning to produce a range of responses and use difficult follow-up questions to challenge the more able learners), and by **assessment** (learners are assessed on an on-going basis so that teaching, and the other methods of differentiation, can be continuously adjusted according to the learners' needs).

(e.g. additional or more challenging tasks) for those that are finishing exercises early.

Examples of strategies can include a lecturer providing more one-to-one feedback to learners during group work or exercises for those struggling with new concepts while other learners continue working on the set exercises, checking learning and providing similar exercises to learners that have understood the new concepts so as to ensure the learning is secured and providing extension activities, with more challenging content, for learners that have completed the set exercises early.

More immediate differentiation strategies can include asking undirected and directed questions and follow-up questions during lectures and discussions. For instance, undirected questions allow learners to volunteer responses, while directed questions ask a specific learner a question. Follow-up questions can be used once a response has been given to reframe and simplify the question where a learner's response is incorrect or ineffective or to ask a more challenging question where the learner has answered correctly or to a high standard.

In the former case, the learner has another opportunity to provide the correct answer, while in the latter case, the learner is stretched and required to think harder about the response. In both cases, if the follow-up questions are used effectively, the learner should be fully engaged and their confidence ought to increase, which should in turn increase motivation and likelihood of future engagement in question and answer sessions.

In some cases, learners may have physical disabilities, learning disabilities, learning difficulties or medical conditions that hinder their engagement and progress in a session or during the course. Identifying these factors and accommodating them through planning for and implementing reasonable adjustments is likely to increase learner engagement and motivation during sessions and the course.

(e) Reasonable adjustments

A reasonable adjustment is any action that helps to reduce the effect of a disability or difficulty that places the learner at a substantial disadvantage in an assessment situation, without prejudicing or compromising the reliability or validity of assessment outcomes or giving the learner an assessment advantage over other learners undertaking the same or similar assessments. A reasonable adjustment is agreed at the pre-assessment stage.

Awarding organisations normally expect learning providers to have drafted and implemented a reasonable adjustments policy and procedure. Reproduced below is a table from an awarding organisation outlining reasonable adjustments that its centres[14] can make, with and without permission.

Key:

Centre - Reasonable adjustment permitted at the discretion of the centre
SV - Consult Standards Verifier for permission
AO - Apply to the awarding organisation for permission

Reasonable adjustment	Assessments NOT taken under examination conditions	Assessments taken under examination conditions
Extra time up to 25%	Centre	SV
Extra time in excess of 25%	Centre	AO
Supervised rest breaks	Centre	AO
Change in the organisation of assessment room	Centre	Centre

---

[14] A Centre is a learning provider that is running the awarding organisation's courses.

Separate accommodation within the centre	Centre	AO
Taking the assessment at an alternative venue	Centre	AO
Use of coloured overlays, low vision aids, tinted spectacles, CCTV and OCR scanners	SV	AO
Use of assistive software	AO	AO
Use of bilingual and bilingual translation dictionaries	Centre	Centre
Assessment Material in enlarged format	Centre	AO
Assessment material in Braille	AO	AO
Language modified assessment material	SV	AO
Assessment material in British Sign Language (BSL)	AO	AO
Assessment material on coloured paper	Centre	Centre
Assessment material in audio format	Centre	SV
Use of ICT	SV	SV
Responses using electronic devices	SV	SV
Responses in BSL	AO	AO
Responses in Braille	AO	AO
Reader	SV	SV
Scribe	SV	AO
BSL/English interpreter	SV	AO

Prompter	SV	AO
Practical assistant	SV	AO
Transcriber	SV	AO
Other	AO	AO

Table: Reasonable adjustments permissions table

Here is a list of reasonable adjustments that a learning provider can make, subject to funding and resources (extracts adapted from *Disability Rights UK Factsheet F11*):

(i) General adjustments

- Access to relevant learning provider documents in the disabled learner's preferred format. (e.g. equal opportunities policy, students' handbook, evacuation and safety procedures)
- Disability equality and impairment specific awareness training for staff
- Staff and students who know about the disabled learner's impairment should have sufficient information and awareness about the adjustments they need
- Adequate financial support to cover any extra costs
- Access to all learning provider facilities
- Support and information before and during the admissions process
- Additional time to complete coursework, assignments, assessments and possibly the entire course
- Study skills support
- Support using the learning resource centre or library, e.g. extended book loans, or help with locating and retrieving books and articles

(ii) General access arrangements

- Disabled learners may need extra time or opportunities to take rest breaks during exams
- Disabled learners may need exam papers in their preferred format
- If disabled learners use assistive technology on their course, they should be able to use it for their exams, e.g. computer equipment, specialist software, together with assistance from a reader or a scribe. There should be technical support on hand in case there are any problems with equipment
- Disabled learners may need to use a separate room so that they are not disturbed by other candidates, and other candidates are not disturbed by them
- Disabled learners may need assistance from another person as a prompter, a scribe (amanuensis) or as a reader
- A disable learner's assistant should have time before the exam to get used to their role, the style and format of the test and any subject- related issues.

(iii) Impairment-specific adjustments

Autism or Asperger syndrome

- Immediate access to pastoral support, e.g. a particular staff member disabled learners can go to with any concern
- Dedicated support worker
- Staff to have awareness training
- Specialist tuition support, e.g. language skills or structuring work
- Materials in literal language, including exam papers
- Special photocopying arrangements
- Digital recorder for recording lectures, notes, etc
- Extra time immediately after group sessions to check understanding
- Extra time to read, understand, and produce answers in exams

- Alternative ways of completing team work
- Support worker to act as a mediator for team work
- To have the same information conveyed in more than one way, e.g. verbally and in writing
- Time to get used to the site
- Preparation for changes of routine, e.g. around deadlines and exam time
- Use of a separate room with an invigilator
- Exam paper written on plain paper in one colour
- Use of a prompter to keep learners focused during exams
- Word processing facilities if motor control is impaired

Blind or visual impairments

- Time to get used to the site
- Support teacher or worker, or a sighted guide
- Personal reader to read course material and exam questions
- Scribes, amanuenses or note-takers to take notes in lectures and dictate answers in exams
- Large print, tape or Braille transcription services
- Handouts and booklists in advance for transcription
- Course material in Braille or in large print, audio format, or via email and exam papers in learners' preferred format
- Digital recorder for recording lectures, notes, etc
- Audio description of visual props used in lectures (or alternative methods of teaching)
- Arrangements for practical and field work
- Assistive technology, e.g. closed-circuit television, computers with speech synthesisers and magnification, Braille note-takers, text scanners, etc
- Use of assistive technology in exams
- Private study area in the library, longer book loans and special arrangements for photocopying
- Exercise area for learners' guide dog
- Good lighting, adequate signs and good colour contrasts on signs and buildings
- Taking exams in a separate room with an invigilator

- Extra time to read, understand, and produce answers in exams
- All exam invigilators to be aware of disabled learner's impairment so they can give time warnings and tell them when to stop writing.

Deaf or hearing impairments

- Human aid to communicate, e.g. sign language interpreter or lip-speaker and signing of exam questions
- Qualified support teacher or tutor, e.g. for language tuition and concept support
- Note-takers
- Remote captioning e.g. using Skype to access a palantypist
- Changing the language of exam papers if the disabled learner is pre-lingually deaf
- Induction loop system in lecture halls and seminar rooms
- Radio or infrared microphone system
- Textphone (e.g. minicom) at home and/or somewhere easily accessible at the learning provider
- For learning provider staff to receive deaf awareness training
- All exam invigilators to be aware of the learner's impairment so they can give time warnings and tell them when to stop writing
- For people disabled learners have a lot of contact with to take British Sign Language (BSL) classes
- Digital recorder and/or copy-typist to record lectures
- Covering the cost of photocopying course materials
- Software to help with English, particularly grammar
- Flashing light or vibrating pad for the fire alarm
- Local Authority support services for disabled/deaf or hearing impaired people
- Video materials to have subtitles
- Use of a separate room, with an invigilator
- Extra time to read, understand, and produce answers in exams.

Learning difficulties

- To be treated with respect as an individual, without staff being directive, patronising or making assumptions about what learners with learning difficulties know and what they can do
- Course materials in plain English or with symbols
- Extra time to put together responses
- Independent advocacy services
- Support worker
- Clear explanation of specific tasks and any changes of routine.

Medical conditions

- Alternative arrangements for work and deadlines if fatigue, stress and effects of medication are an issue
- Timetable planning to avoid fatigue and problem environments
- Digital recorder for recording lectures, notes, etc.
- Arrangements to meet specific dietary needs, e.g. use of a fridge
- Rest room on campus or site
- Medical support and emergency arrangements
- Place of privacy to take medication and assistance if required
- Ongoing dialogue with staff if learners have a hidden and/or fluctuating condition
- Contact from staff during any periods of time away from studies
- Flexibility in attendance and punctuality if treatments or therapies are tightly scheduled
- Designated parking space
- Awareness among staff of the learner's condition
- Maintenance of confidentiality regarding learner's condition

- Specialist or adapted computer equipment, e.g. a screen filter or monitor without flicker if the learner has have photosensitive epilepsy
- Provision of snacks during exams
- All exam invigilators to be aware of a learner's impairment so they know what to do in a medical emergency
- Supervised rest breaks during exams.

Mental health condition

- Timetable planning and help with a learner's work programme to deal with stress. This may include limiting the number of exams in a day or week
- Extra support and help with planning before or during exam and assessment periods
- Exam officers to be aware that problems may arise during exam periods
- Support from welfare and counselling staff
- Named contact to go to for support when necessary
- Academic staff to be clear about what they expect from the learner
- Flexibility in attendance and punctuality if treatments or therapies are tightly scheduled or during times when difficulties are worse than usual
- Computer equipment to enable learners to study at home
- Quiet room to rest in
- Contact from staff during any periods of time away from studies
- Maintenance of confidentiality about learners' mental health condition
- Sufficient information and awareness among staff who do know about learners' difficulties, to prevent major misconceptions
- Supervised rest breaks during exams
- Prompter to keep learners focused in exams

Physical impairments

- Physically accessible classrooms, exam rooms, study spaces, toilets, catering and leisure facilities and telephones
- Personal assistants or mobility helpers
- Adapted furniture for studying at home or college and use of these in exams
- Powered wheelchair and facilities for charging it
- Assistive technology such as a switch-operated or voice-activated computer.
- Use of assistive technology in exams
- Scanner
- Typing or transcription services
- Digital recorder for recording lectures, notes, etc.
- Scribes, amanuenses or note-takers for lectures and exams
- Support for practical and field work
- Particular travel arrangements
- Parking space on campus
- Timetable planning to ensure accessibility and avoid long distances
- Additional time at mealtimes for medical needs
- Rest room on campus
- Well-ventilated classrooms if heat leads to discomfort
- Extra time for course work and exams, depending on learners' method of communication and working
- Use of a separate room, with an invigilator, if using equipment or taking frequent rests because of fatigue
- Supervised rest breaks during exams

Specific learning difficulties (e.g. dyslexia, dyspraxia, dyscalculia)

- Specialist tuition support, e.g. language skills or structuring work
- Support with identifying the most relevant books and chapters to read

- Assistive technology such as a computer with dictionary explanations software or a screen reader
- Use of assistive technology in exams
- Use of a separate exam room, with an invigilator
- Digital recorder
- Use of a scanner
- Handouts and booklists in advance of classes
- Handouts and exam papers in preferred format, e.g. on tape or on different coloured paper
- Special photocopying arrangements
- Scribes, amanuenses or note-takers, proof-reader, support worker, and use of amanuenses in exams
- Extra time to read, understand and prepare answers
- Use of literal language and keeping oral instructions simple and concise
- Extra time after tutorials to check understanding
- Exam papers printed on coloured paper or printed in ink other than blue or black
- Use of coloured filters or overlays
- Use of coloured pens (other than blue or black)
- Oral examinations instead of, or in addition to, the written examination.

Speech, language and communication impairments

- Modified assessment arrangements for any oral exams and presentations or group work
- Timetables to include longer tutorial and seminar sessions
- Advice and guidance from a speech and language therapist
- Textphone at home and/or somewhere easily accessible at the learning provider
- Communication aid or interpreter
- Communication board or computer with a speech synthesiser

As a lecturer, teaching, learning and assessment strategies need to be informed by the nature and extent of reasonable adjustments made for learners. These may vary significantly from one group / class to another. Consequently, schemes of work and lesson plans may need some amendments to take account of these learners and periodic meetings might be required to ensure that the arrangement is working effectively and that all learners are making the necessary progress. In some cases the adjustments made to teaching, learning and assessment strategies, where they also impact on learners without disabilities or learning difficulties, could benefit all learners. Examples include the following:

(a) subtitled videos for deaf learners might also prove useful to learners with English as a second language, particularly where participants in the videos have a strong regional accent or are speaking too fast;

(b) increased use of short sentences and more visual aids in sessions for dyslexic learners may also benefit learners that have short attention spans and prefer visual learning; and

(c) learning alongside learners with disabilities and learning difficulties should improve awareness of how to deal with such issues when learners are completing assignments with tasks relating to equality and diversity, attending job interviews when questioned about equality and diversity and when entering a workplace with people from diverse backgrounds and a range of skills and abilities.

Learners without disabilities and learning difficulties need to be made aware of the reasonable adjustments being made for learners with disabilities or learning difficulties and their rationale, especially where the disability is not obvious and the adjustments can be perceived as providing an unfair advantage to a learner with a disability or learning difficulty.

For instance, dyslexic learners receiving extra time for examinations could require more awareness raising for learners without such learning difficulties than a blind learner requiring a reader, scribe and 100% extra time for an examination. Dyslexia and its impact is less obvious to learners who have no experience of it than understanding that a blind learner requires a range of reasonable adjustments, since the disability is more apparent and those without the disability can more readily sympathise with the need for such adjustments.

(f) Teaching and learning styles and varied assessment methods

The concept of learning styles considers that people learn in different ways and have a set of preferences in the way they learn. For instance, 'VARK' is often used to outline the different learning styles. VARK stands for Visual (learning by seeing), Auditory (learning by listening), Read and write (learning by reading and writing / making or taking notes) and Kinaesthetic (learning by doing). If you are not sure about your learning style and preferences, you can complete a *VARK questionnaire* as a starting point to outline your learning style preferences. Some examples of these questionnaires can be found online.

Being aware that learners have different learning styles and preferences and that these could vary depending on the nature of the subject (e.g. law is more difficult to teach with visual aids than ICT or engineering) should inform teaching, learning and assessment strategies, ensuring that they are more balanced and inclusive. Ideally, learners should be able to engage with the entire range of learning styles during their course, since higher education, professional courses and employment at some point require competence in the entire range of learning styles, although the degree of competence or proficiency may vary from subject to subject and sector to sector and even within roles and tasks and over time.

Assessment methods tend to reflect learning styles. For instance, presentations tend to require more visual and kinaesthetic elements than read write elements, while role play requires more auditory and kinaesthetic elements. Learners with dyslexia and learners whose first language is not English may perform better when engaged with presentations and producing posters, since both focus more on visual elements than read and write elements. Such learners might experience difficulties when asked to complete a detailed written report.

Assessments that do not provide a variety of assessment methods and programmes that do not vary learning styles potentially disadvantage learners, since further, higher and professional education and most areas of employment expect employees to be proficient across the range, as mentioned earlier (albeit to varying degrees, depending on the profession or job role). For instance, a Solicitor is likely to be expected to have a high level of proficiency in read, write and auditory elements, while a test engineer is likely to be expected to have high levels of proficiency in kinaesthetic and visual elements).

Awarding organisations normally expect a learning provider to use a range of assessment methods when delivering internally assessed programmes, particularly vocational programmes. Inspection bodies also expect a range of activities taking place in a session, as may learning providers when undertaking their own lesson observations. Sustained learner engagement is more likely where activities and methods of engagement are varied, such as receiving presentations, taking part in role play, group work, completing written exercises, discussions, question and answer sessions and preparing and giving a mini-presentation. These require the entire range of VARK elements. The extent to which these and other assessment methods are used in teaching and learning can vary according to the nature of the subject or task.

2. Strengths and limitations of teaching and learning approaches used in a particular area when meeting individual learner needs

(a) Teaching approaches

Each subject tends to share a common teaching approach with other subjects and also includes approaches that are specific to that subject or that category of subjects.

(i) Business Studies

Teaching approach	Strengths	Limitations
Lectures	• Provides a means to disseminate detailed information in a short-time. • Allows lecturers to make the information and concepts more 'digestible' than textbooks, including current examples.	• May not appeal to all learners, depending on their learning styles and preferences. • Lecturers need to keep up-to-date with sector developments in order to make lectures engaging. • Learner interaction can be limited if lectures do not include questions and answers, discussion and other activities.
PowerPoint Presentations	• If used effectively, including integration of multimedia, can maintain learner engagement.	• 'death by PowerPoint' – it can be over-used. • Lecturers need to be skilled in making effective use of PowerPoint and only

		use it as one among many teaching tools, otherwise learners are likely to go off-task.
Questions and answers	• Effective use of undirected, directed and follow-up questions should ensure full class engagement.	• It requires learners to have sufficient confidence to engage fully. • Learners with English as a second language may need more time to process the questions before responding, which could lead to embarrassment.
Discussion	• Should lead to deeper learning and understanding of the subject, providing opportunities for a range of learner views to be shared.	• It requires learners to have a degree of underpinning knowledge and understanding. • There is the risk of some learners dominating discussions to the detriment of others, particularly where English is not their first language and fluency is limited.
Live case studies	• Learners can examine a business as a situation develops and monitor it on a weekly basis. This increases realism. • Learners are likely to be more motivated, especially if there is media reporting of the organisation and its situation,	• There may be insufficient data or information to undertake detailed or meaningful analysis. • It might take a long time for the situation to develop further or to its logical conclusion, by which time learners are likely to lose focus.

	including multi-media and social media based reports (e.g. You Tube, Facebook, blogs), which learners tend to be more comfortable engaging with.	
Case studies	• Traditional case studies provide complete coverage of a situation, since the event has occurred and the matter is concluded, and so can be fully examined (e.g. Barclays Bank's fund raising during the 2008 financial crisis and its current financial position in 2015). • Learners gain a practical insight into application of business concepts, theories and market conditions to an organisation.	• The case study may be dated and not as exciting as a breaking story or live case study. • The case study might not appeal to the interests of all learners, so a variety of case studies may need to be used, which requires more planning and effort by the lecturer.
Exemplar material (e.g. critically reviewing previously completed learner work)	• Learners can examine and critically review with the lecturer, the strengths and weaknesses of a completed response and thereby be clear about the standard expected of them. • Exemplar responses can be	• Less able or less motivated learners might become demotivated and suffer from reduced confidence due to the task ahead of them. • A lot of time and effort will need to be expended to unpack how the previous learner reached the

	used as part of skills development (e.g. essay / assignment writing skills).	response, especially where it is of a detailed/complex nature or of high quality.
Research skills	• Developing these skills early is likely to benefit learners across all their programme and not just the units that focus on undertaking a research project.	• Research skills take time to learn, and learners need to experiment and experience failure or disappointment in the outcomes of their 'experiments' before they can apply research skills effectively to related research project units or assignments that require a lot of research. • There may not be sufficient time in the standard timetable to develop research skills. Additional workshops might prove necessary, which have cost and resource implications for the learning provider and loss of social time for learners.
Facilitated group work	• Paired and group work provide opportunities to share a range of views and personal and professional experiences. • It provides opportunities for peer learning and support, which is less intimidating	• Groups take time to settle down. • There may be personal tensions and conflicts between some of the group members, which could reduce its productivity and effectiveness. • There is a risk of 'free-riding', where a

	than asking for help from the lecturer. • It develops transferrable employability skills. • As a group, learners may become more confident to contribute their views, since an incorrect response is shared collectively by the group rather than being focused on one person alone.	learner decides to contribute less than other members or not at all, expecting other team members to complete their part of the task.
Facilitated role play	• Lecturers set the boundaries and scope of the role play and allocate the roles. The role play provides an opportunity to gain practical experience of a simulated situation. • Other learners can critically examine the role plays and learn from each other.	• Learners require some practice to undertake the role play effectively. • There are a limited range of topics and situations that lend themselves readily to role play.
Post business related visit debriefing / reflection	• Learners are able to reflect on real life business situations, which assists in internalising related business concepts.	• Business-related visits provide limited opportunities / a snapshot of business concepts in practice.

Good practice examples of teaching Business Studies (extracts from Ofsted inspections and/or related publications)

- "Lessons were well planned and clear learning objectives were linked to detailed schemes of work. Teachers used their excellent subject knowledge to plan and teach lessons with a strong emphasis on learning. Such lessons, often conducted at a very good pace, engaged students very successfully." (01/2008)

- "A good range of starter activities, such as quizzes, true/false questions and 'bingo' style games to test students' knowledge of definitions, provided prompt and purposeful starts to lessons. One key feature of many lessons was to introduce activities to help maintain students' motivation and a good pace of learning; this included group work, working in pairs, practical exercises, presentations, visiting speakers, business games and role play." (*Ibid.*)

- "Teachers planned and managed group work effectively. They had a very good rapport with their students and they had thought carefully about the impact of such work on their learning. The main strengths of the lessons involving group work students' effective work in a cooperative and competitive business environment. They listened carefully to each other's ideas and presented arguments, often backed up by examples, to reach a valid conclusion." (*Ibid.*)

- "Imaginative teaching engaged students and used up to date and relevant business examples. For example, a lesson on ratio analysis was made far more meaningful for students by using real data. Students were split into three groups, each having the data for a different branch of a company. Each group had to prepare a presentation to demonstrate that they could analyse the data using various ratios and use the information to make decisions about the performance of their branch." (*Ibid.*)

- "The professional presentation standards of teachers' worksheets and assignment briefs met students' needs very effectively and contributed to the sense of high expectations. In one college, teachers were responsible for particular modules and developed assignments, resources and assessments for the rest of the teaching team to use. They evaluated each other's materials and suggested improvements. In three of the colleges visited, key notes and revision material had been developed by teachers and students as podcasts so that students could access these with their MP3 players. The students were very enthusiastic about this alternative way of learning that they could do anytime and anywhere." (*Ibid.*)

- "Teachers drew effectively on students' own experience of work to illustrate theory. The survey also found good examples of local business people contributing to students' learning by discussing their experiences and providing feedback to students on their work." (*Ibid.*)

- "Teachers used PowerPoint effectively to present information and often made links to relevant websites and topical issues." (*Ibid.*)

- "Teachers' feedback on written work was thorough and, in almost all the colleges, gave students clear guidance on what they needed to do to improve." (*Ibid.*)

- "Support for students, both in and outside lessons, was a major strength in the colleges visited." (*Ibid.*)

- "Teachers use a wide range of interesting and appropriate activities that enthuse learners, maintain their interest and prepare them effectively for examinations. Examples from the real world give immediacy and relevance to lessons, such as the reasons for a major supermarket locating in nearby Hulme." (11/2009)

- "Teachers monitor students' progress thoroughly." (*Ibid.*)

- "Assessors use innovative approaches and well-planned assessment activities to build and further extend apprentices' vocational knowledge and their application of skills. They provide accurate, purposeful and timely feedback to apprentices on their assessments, both online and in meetings. Apprentices receive highly effective developmental evaluations of their strengths and areas for improvement. They welcome corrections made to their written work regarding spelling, punctuation and grammar and value the improvements that arise as a result." (03/2014)

- "Apprentices develop excellent practical and technical skills through assessors' skilful coaching techniques, imaginative use of virtual learning sites and high quality training away from the workplace." (*Ibid.*)

(ii) Law

Teaching approach	Strengths	Limitations
Lectures	• Provide a means to disseminate detailed information in a short timeframe. • Allows lecturers to make the information and concepts more 'digestible' than textbooks, including current examples and own observations.	• May not appeal to all learners, depending on their learning styles and preferences. • Lecturers need to keep up-to-date with sector developments in order to make lectures engaging. • Learner interaction can be limited if lectures do not include questions and answers,

		discussion and other activities.
PowerPoint Presentations	• If used effectively, including integration of multimedia, where appropriate, it can maintain learner engagement.	• 'death by PowerPoint' – it can be over-used. • Lecturers need to be skilled in making effective use of PowerPoint and only use it as one among many teaching tools, otherwise learners are likely to go off-task.
Questions and answers	• Effective use of undirected, directed and follow-up questions should ensure full class engagement.	• It requires learners to have sufficient confidence to engage fully. • Learners with English as a second language may need more time to process the question before responding, which could lead to embarrassment.
Discussion	• Should lead to deeper learning and understanding of the subject, providing opportunities for a range of learner views to be shared.	• It requires learners to have a degree of underpinning knowledge and understanding. • There is the risk of some learners dominating discussions to the detriment of others, particularly where English is not their first language and fluency is limited.
Interpretation of legislation	• Learners understand how to	• Most courses below

	navigate and correctly apply legislation to a given scenario or situation. This is an important transferrable skill for further study and related employment.	undergraduate level do not provide detailed techniques to interpret legislation, thereby equipping learners with basic interpretation skills.
Analysis of case law	• Learners understand the reasons for the decisions and the influences of precedent (i.e. decisions on similar or same points of law from higher courts, which are influential on lower courts). This is an important transferrable skill for further study and related employment.	• Courses below undergraduate level do not examine in any detail the decisions of judges, which can run into tens of pages and refer to judgements from other judges in higher courts.
Essay writing skills	• Legal essay structure and correct citation of cases and application of legislation are distinct from standard essay writing techniques. Learners taught these techniques are in a better position to develop an effective argument / submission.	• Essay writing skills do not provide the range of skills needed in practice to formulate, present and follow through with an argument or submission in a court or during pre-court legal proceedings. Essays are of little or no use in practice. For instance, during the Legal Practice Course (for

		prospective solicitors) or the Bar Professional Training Course (for prospective barristers), there are no essays, but instead preparation of papers, opinions, advocacy and negotiation.
Facilitating / deciding on Moot competitions (i.e. 2-4 learners arguing on a point of law)	• These provide opportunities to practice submissions / arguments on points of law (often in the context of a case going to appeal). This provides direct transferrable skills, if applied correctly. • If set-up effectively, it could provide those intending to obtain work placements or holiday work in solicitors' firms or barristers' chambers with some better opportunities, since competition is fierce in the legal sector. At undergraduate level, barristers' chambers normally expect to see a track record of successful participation in	• It requires a lot of preparation, access to sufficient learning resources and a degree of experience / expertise from the lecturer overseeing this process. • At below undergraduate level, these are likely to be fairly superficial.

	mooting competitions, since the skills are directly transferrable to advocacy.	
Facilitating / deciding on debates over points of law	• These provide underpinning advocacy-style skills, which are transferrable for further study or for a better understanding of law and for practice. • This should provide a deeper understanding of law in practice and having to defend one's position should improve reasoning, analytical and evaluative skills, which can be transferred to essay writing.	• Learners require a lot of training and practice to develop effective debating skills on points of law.
Post court related visit debriefing / reflection	• This puts things into context, relating back to elements or topics in the course (e.g. watching a criminal trial at the 'Old Bailey') will provide a better idea of the role of QCs (senior barristers) and barristers in the legal profession, the role of the jury and how	• At below undergraduate level, the case being observed may be too technical, or of little interest or the visit may occur in an on-going case, with the opportunity of only a short snap-shot of proceedings (learners may not understand the

		submissions are made and evidence used. Lecturers can unpack and relate the learner experience to topics in their course. • Watching a short one or two day trial from start to finish should provide good insight into court proceedings and different roles in practice. This will make it easier for the lecturer to relate what learners have seen back to the topics on the course.	background of the case or the current arguments being made). This will make it difficult for lecturers to relate back what learners have seen to their topic. Moreover, seating is limited, notes are not allowed and so lecturers may not be attending the hearing that learners have attended, thereby reducing the effectiveness of post-visit debriefing and reflection.

Good practice examples of teaching Law (extracts from Ofsted inspections and/or related publications)

- "Questioning is used well to promote learning and to assess students' knowledge, for example in a Year 13 law lesson where the teacher probed students' understanding of the use of case law through sophisticated questioning." (01/2014b)

- "Visits are made to ... courts" (09/2011)

- "Lessons were well planned and clear learning objectives were linked to detailed schemes of work. Teachers used their excellent subject knowledge to plan and teach lessons with a strong emphasis on learning. Such lessons, often conducted at a very good pace, engaged students very successfully." (01/2008)

- "Teachers had high expectations of what their students could do in lessons. Their very effective questioning deepened students' understanding and skills in analysis and evaluation. They were often skilled in asking follow-up questions and developing students' confidence, which encouraged very good contributions to discussions. In one A-level law lesson, for example, students researched cases to illustrate aspects and principles of causation in criminal law and prepared a presentation on the facts, decisions and legal principles from the case studies. There was some very good discussion of legal causation. The teacher asked searching questions, and the students in turn asked well considered questions of the teacher and each other. They showed a good understanding of the law and confidence in presenting clear and well-argued cases." (*Ibid.*)

- *"Realistic simulation to develop students' understanding of how theory fits into the real world*: Students had the opportunity to engage in a realistic simulation of court practice in the local Crown Court. They made an introductory visit to observe proceedings, which was then followed up by a two-day programme where they took over the Court premises for a simulation. A working judge presided over the proceedings. Students were given the details of actual cases, which were made anonymous, to prepare for their roles as prosecutor, defence and jury. Students were highly motivated by the event, which had been developed as a result of the good working relationships between the legal staff of the college and the local law society." (*Ibid.*)

(iii) ICT

Teaching approach	Strengths	Limitations
Lectures	• Provide a means to disseminate detailed information in a short timeframe. • Allows lecturers to make the information and concepts more 'digestible' than textbooks, including current examples and own observations.	• May not appeal to all learners, depending on their learning styles and preferences. • Lecturers need to keep up-to-date with sector developments in order to make lectures engaging. • Learner interaction can be limited if lectures do not include questions and answers, discussion and other activities.
PowerPoint Presentations	• If used effectively, including integration of multimedia, where appropriate, it can maintain learner engagement.	• 'death by PowerPoint' – it can be over-used. • Lecturers need to be skilled in making effective use of PowerPoint and only use it as one among many teaching tools, otherwise learners are likely to go off-task.
Questions and answers	• Effective use of undirected, directed and follow-up questions should ensure full class engagement.	• It requires learners to have sufficient confidence to engage fully. • Learners with English as a second language may need more

		time to process the question before responding, which could lead to embarrassment.
Discussion	• Should lead to deeper learning and understanding of the subject, providing opportunities for a range of learner views to be shared.	• It requires learners to have a degree of underpinning knowledge and understanding. • There is the risk of some learners dominating discussions to the detriment of others, particularly where English is not their first language and fluency is limited.
Instructions on using software	• Being provided with step-by-step instructions on how to use the software and its features effectively reduces the time spent on reading manuals and experimenting. Lecturers are more likely to know the software features most relevant to the course and assessment criteria, thereby making the learning directly relevant to the	• Without repeated and recent practice, learners are likely to forget more complex techniques, especially if they were dependent on the lecturer's instructions in class. • The more dependent learners are on the step-by-step instructions provided by lecturers, the less likely they are to retain and repeat that knowledge on their own, unless they have

	course and assessments.		practiced on their own and learnt
	• Learning by doing / kinaesthetic learning is more relevant to ICT, especially for further study, where software programming may be involved or use of the software being demonstrated in the lesson (e.g. website design) or in future practice. Even if the software used in the future is made by a different software company, the underpinning principles and techniques are likely to be transferrable (although the steps used to apply the technique may need some getting used to).		those techniques without further assistance.
	• Learners that are already familiar with the software could, with the agreement of the lecturer, assist other learners, thereby developing transferrable skills and re-enforcing their existing		• Some learners may already be familiar with the software and some or most of its features, thereby making the session(s) less relevant. Lecturers will need to consider extension activities or other activities to ensure that learners are fully engaged and remain motivated.

	learning (explaining a technique to another person tends to be harder than learning the technique for oneself, so being able to explain it should re-enforce one's own understand of the technique).	
Instructions on programming software	• If the lecturer has recent experience of using the programming language being taught, they can assist learners to find more effective and efficient routes to applying the programming language.	• Very careful planning is required to ensure that all learners' needs are being met. Some may already be familiar with the programming language, some may struggle with it and others may prefer a different programming language.
Instructions on hardware installation	• This provides hands-on experience of installing hardware, which should develop transferrable skills for further related study and employment.	• Depending on the type and level of programme, the resourcing requirements may be high. (Since computer technology changes every 6 months; purchasing the latest hardware may prove difficult).
Examining problems that require a software solution	• This should develop problem-solving skills and	• It is difficult to find a problem that requires a

	transferrable skills for further related study and employment.	software solution that appeals to the interests of the learner. Some of the more interesting problems may require complex software solutions that are beyond the scope of the programme or the current abilities of the learner.
Practical demonstrations of software and hardware application	• This should make the programme 'come to life', demonstrating real life use of software and hardware.	• It is difficult to find examples that are interesting and may require a visit to a company or facility where the application being used is interesting and fully engages and inspires learners (the development of advanced robotics is a good example).

Good practice examples of teaching ICT (extracts from Ofsted inspections and/or related publications)

- "Tutors are very knowledgeable and experienced within the information technology industry. They use their knowledge very well to relate their classroom teaching to real life situations." (11/2013)

- "Tutors have a good rapport with apprentices, using humour well to teach very abstract topics." (*Ibid.*)

- "Apprentices develop skills in, for example, programming and software development, configuring networks and web development, and enjoy the challenging tasks they are set." (*Ibid.*)

- "Classroom-based sessions have a good balance of theoretical and practical activity." (*Ibid.*)

- "Tutors are well aware of learners' individual needs and they plan lessons using carefully chosen activities and questioning techniques." (*Ibid.*)

- "Inspirational teaching, learning and assessment engage apprentices exceptionally well and lead to excellent attainment." (*Ibid.*)

- "Tutors are skilled at helping apprentices to develop personal, learning, and thinking skills well." (*Ibid.*)

- "Teaching, learning, and assessment highlight the importance of spelling and grammar. Tutors reinforce skilfully to the apprentices the importance of using grammatically correct English by producing assignments and handouts with errors for apprentices to correct." (*Ibid.*)

- "Assessors make excellent use of questioning techniques to enable apprentices to demonstrate their very high levels of knowledge and skills. This also supports development of independent learning skills. Apprentices are able to link on- and off-the-job training well through the development of technical terms and understanding of theoretical aspects." (*Ibid.*)

- "Tutors and assessors provide good written and verbal feedback on assessments promptly, which helps apprentices to improve the standards of their work. The marking of assessed work provides constructive feedback to support further development of knowledge and skills. Verbal feedback during lessons is highly effective." (*Ibid.*)

- "Apprentices demonstrate good understanding of equality and diversity. Their portfolios include various scenarios to encourage them to develop their knowledge of equality and diversity. Almost all assessors routinely integrate equality and diversity in assessment and reviews. Examples include how to tackle bullying, harassment, discrimination, and consideration of accessibility for wheelchair users as part of writing software packages to control automatic doors." (*Ibid.*)

(iv) Beauty Therapy

Teaching approach	Strengths	Limitations
Lectures	<ul><li>Provide a means to disseminate detailed information in a short timeframe.</li><li>Allows lecturers to make the information and concepts more 'digestible' than textbooks, including current examples and own observations.</li></ul>	<ul><li>May not appeal to all learners, depending on their learning styles and preferences.</li><li>Lecturers need to keep up-to-date with sector developments in order to make lectures engaging.</li><li>Learner interaction can be limited if lectures do not include questions and answers, discussion and other activities.</li></ul>
PowerPoint Presentations	<ul><li>If used effectively, including integration of</li></ul>	<ul><li>'death by PowerPoint' – it can be over-used.</li></ul>

	multimedia, where appropriate, it can maintain learner engagement.	• Lecturers need to be skilled in making effective use of PowerPoint and only use it as one among many teaching tools, otherwise learners are likely to go off-task.
Questions and answers	• Effective use of undirected, directed and follow-up questions should ensure full class engagement.	• It requires learners to have sufficient confidence to engage fully. • Learners with English as a second language may need more time to process the question before responding, which could lead to embarrassment.
Discussion	• Should lead to deeper learning and understanding of the subject, providing opportunities for a range of learner views to be shared.	• It requires learners to have a degree of underpinning knowledge and understanding. • There is the risk of some learners dominating discussions to the detriment of others, particularly where English is not their first language and fluency is limited.
Demonstration of Beauty techniques	• Given the health and safety issues involved in most beauty techniques	• Some techniques are resource intensive, and specialist

	and treatments, detailed demonstrations of how the techniques are to be used are essential to ensuring the health and safety of current or future clients.	equipment may need to be hired, together with a willing client or learner to undergo the treatment. These are more difficult to source where techniques or treatments are of a permanent or semi-permanent nature (e.g. semi-permanent make-up).
Overseeing and, where necessary, providing guidance on Beauty treatments on other learners and clients	• This provides assurances that health and safety protocols are being followed and the treatments are being applied effectively. • Clients are also reassured that they are not only receiving a free or low cost treatment, but that it is of an acceptable standard. • Formative feedback (or being given tips on how to improve the application of the treatment) should lead to deeper learning.	• Frequent feedback and tips during treatments may reduce learner confidence. This could also reduce the confidence of fellow learners and clients.
Overseeing roles in a beauty salon situation	• This should provide learners with a real life context to their programme, especially where	• This requires a great deal of investment in resources.

	real clients are seen. • This should develop directly relevant transferrable skills for employment in a beauty salon.	• It also requires clients to attend the beauty salon, which is more likely during evenings, leading to a long day for learners at the learning provider. This may prove difficult where learners have other commitments.

Good practice examples of teaching Beauty Therapy (extracts from Ofsted inspections and/or related publications)

- "Motivated tutors have high expectations, which they share with students constantly. They pepper their teaching with industrial comparisons and scenarios, inspiring students to match commercial time restraints, protocols and professional standards." (Ofsted; 01/2014)

- "Tutors plan effectively a particularly wide range of activities that promote the acquisition of knowledge." (*Ibid.*)

- "Learning materials are of a high standard, well presented and designed to engage and motivate students." (*Ibid.*)

- "In the majority of lessons, tutors use well-phrased questions to extend themes, prompt discussion and assess students' understanding." (*Ibid.*)

- "Tutors know their students extremely well and adapt lesson content to meet their needs. Students who were preparing hesitantly for their first external clients benefited from the tutor spending additional time providing detailed guidance on process and practice." (*Ibid.*)

- "Beauty therapy students appreciate the college's progressive attitude, inviting a cosmetic surgeon to the college as a guest speaker." (*Ibid.*)

- "Frequent progress reviews record explicitly the skills and related theoretical principles that students have acquired. Tutors record progress and achievements in language students understand and make use of incremental development targets to move students effectively towards their ultimate goal." (*Ibid.*)

- "Teachers are extremely effective in developing learners' skills and knowledge of key technical aspects of hairdressing, beauty and holistic therapies, such as 'electrical' facials and the elaborate dressing of long hair into avant-garde styles." (03/2014)

- "Teachers plan and deliver a variety of extremely thoughtful and imaginative lessons, such as the use of a popular 'game show' format to learn about essential oils in aromatherapy and mask making for foundation level learners." (*Ibid.*)

- "Teachers reinforce high standards in the salons, and provide exceptional support and care for learners, ensuring they develop consistently safe working practices. (*Ibid.*)

- Teachers provide a high level of support through frequent and expert technical feedback." (*Ibid.*)

- "Teachers ensure a planned, sustained focus on the development of English in lessons. Learners write self-evaluations and develop technical language whilst improving their written English." (*Ibid.*)

- "Teachers focus sharply on the development of learners' employability skills, and this is reflected in their very high standards of client care and retail awareness." (*Ibid.*)

- "Teachers maximise opportunities to develop learners' awareness of highly relevant equality and diversity issues, such as 'body image' and the expanding market of male beauty treatments. They promote very positive relationships between learners who are sensitive to each other's differences." (*Ibid.*)

(v) Science

Teaching approach	Strengths	Limitations
Lectures	• Provide a means to disseminate detailed information in a short timeframe. • Allows lecturers to make the information and concepts more 'digestible' than textbooks, including current examples and own observations.	• May not appeal to all learners, depending on their learning styles and preferences. • Lecturers need to keep up-to-date with sector developments in order to make lectures engaging. • Learner interaction can be limited if lectures do not include questions and answers, discussion and other activities.
PowerPoint Presentations	• If used effectively, including integration of multimedia, where appropriate, it can maintain learner engagement.	• 'death by PowerPoint' – it can be over-used. • Lecturers need to be skilled in making effective use of PowerPoint and only use it as one among many

		teaching tools, otherwise learners are likely to go off-task.
Questions and answers	• Effective use of undirected, directed and follow-up questions should ensure full class engagement.	• It requires learners to have sufficient confidence to engage fully. • Learners with English as a second language may need more time to process the question before responding, which could lead to embarrassment.
Discussion	• Should lead to deeper learning and understanding of the subject, providing opportunities for a range of learner views to be shared.	• It requires learners to have a degree of underpinning knowledge and understanding. • There is the risk of some learners dominating discussions to the detriment of others, particularly where English is not their first language and fluency is limited.
Practical demonstration	• This is important in ensuring that learners know how to conduct the experiments being demonstrated, so that they remain safe and carry out the experiment effectively. • This should increase learner	• This can be resource intensive. • Some of the specialist demonstrations may require visits to professional laboratories. • Some demonstrations, especially those relating to biology, may need to be

	engagement, especially where the outcome of the experiment is unexpected or interesting (e.g. vigorous chemical reactions in a subject like Chemistry).	spread across a number of sessions and therefore require careful planning.
Overseeing and, where necessary, providing guidance on practical experiments	• This should ensure health and safety is maintained and that learners are undertaking the most effective and efficient route to completing the experiment. • Guidance while undertaking the experiment may lead to deeper learning, since feedback is instantaneous and adjustments can be made immediately.	• Too frequent intervention and guidance might reduce learner confidence.

Good practice examples of teaching Science (extracts from Ofsted inspections and/or related publications)

- "In the best science lessons, students work hard and show good levels of application. Tutors use imaginative ways to help students learn. For example, in one particularly effective biology lesson, students used a matching cards activity to reinforce their understanding before working on examination questions. Work booklets across the science subjects are of high quality and give students a good framework for their learning. Experimental work is generally good and is a strong feature of the extended diploma in applied science. Tutors set homework regularly." (Ofsted; 01/2014)

- "Tutors arrange additional support promptly for those students identified through initial assessment as requiring extra help." (*Ibid.*)

- "Science tutors also give students a good awareness of available careers." (*Ibid.*)

- "Assessments are at the right level and help students to understand examination requirements. Work is marked regularly with helpful comments on how to improve. Tutors correct poorly constructed sentences and obvious spelling mistakes in students' work. They promote the correct use of specialist vocabulary effectively, which helps students to perform better in examinations." (*Ibid.*)

- "Teachers bring lessons to life by engaging students in different ways, especially in biology. For example, in a lesson on genetics, the students have to provide meaningful explanations to topics studied such as providing a running commentary to a video clip showing the unzipping of a strand of DNA." (Ofsted; 10/2014)

- "Teachers plan activities very well resulting in students developing good independent research, discussion, experimentation and problem solving skills. For example, in a physics lesson, with minimal help from the teacher, students pooled their resources, successfully designing and building apparatus to measure the energy stored in a capacitor." (*Ibid.*)

- "Teachers help students to make excellent progress by effective use of working in pairs or groups. The students develop their own understanding well by discussing and explaining ideas to their peers, as well as their interpersonal and longer-term employability skills." (*Ibid.*)

- "Teachers set and mark homework regularly and return it promptly with useful, specific comments on what each student needs to do to improve. Their supportive and complimentary comments on good work motivate the students." (*Ibid.*)

- "Teachers provide excellent academic support for students. They are generous with their time outside lessons to help students. Extra support and revision sessions are provided outside timetabled lessons and these, combined with the rigorous monitoring of performance, help to raise students' attainment." (Oftsed; 11/2009)

- "Teachers monitor students' progress rigorously. They closely evaluate students' performance against their target grades. Progress is recorded using an on-line system that students find very useful in helping them to take responsibility for their own learning. Students in need of help are promptly identified and followed up swiftly and relentlessly. Action is consistent and tenacious, and, if appropriate, concerns are referred to the principal who sees students individually." (*Ibid.*)

- "Learners develop sound, safe and confident practical skills in science. Teachers are effective in enabling learners to achieve a deep understanding of the link between theory and practice. During a practical investigation of the chromatography of spinach, learners took part in a dramatic role play, with learners playing the part of different elements, and this deepened their understanding of the experimental process." (03/2014)

- "Teachers check learning frequently through a range of approaches, including excellent question and answer techniques, the use of mini-whiteboards and learners' response cards." (*Ibid.*)

(b) Learning approaches

(i) Teacher-centred approach vs. Learner-centred approach to learning

There has been a move towards learner-centred learning and in most cases learning is given more importance than teaching, especially during Ofsted inspections.

Teacher-centred approach to learning	Learner-centred approach to learning
Teachers are the centre of knowledge, directing learning and controlling learner's access to learning.	Learners construct their own meaning by talking, listening, writing, reading and reflecting on content, ideas, issues and concerns.
Learners are viewed as 'empty' vessels, i.e. not having any relevant prior knowledge or experience of the topic / subject, and so little or no account is taken of relevant prior learning or experience.	Learners' prior knowledge, learning and experience are taken into account.
Assessments take the form of traditional exams.	Assessment is mainly formative in nature, with constructive and continuous feedback (i.e. the focus is on guiding learners to improve and enhance their understanding of the subject and guidance is given how to do this). Summative assessment still plays a role (i.e. grading and stating how well a learner has performed at a particular point), but this role stops short of formative assessment.

Teaching is focused on delivering to the 'middle', i.e. average learners.	It is recognised that learners have different learning styles and preferences and this is encouraged and supported. Teaching and learning is differentiated (i.e. it caters for learners with below average, average and above average aptitudes for the subject).
Information is organised and presented predominantly by the teacher.	The learner is given direct access to multiple sources of information and assisted in solving problems / completing tasks making informed / effective use of those resources.
There is a focus on lower order thinking skills (e.g. 'recall', 'identify', 'define') and memorisation of abstract and isolated facts, figures and formulas.	There is an emphasis on inter-disciplinary knowledge, encouragement of higher order thinking and information skills (e.g. problem-solving, access, organisation, interpretation and communication of knowledge). Learners work with teachers to select learning goals and objectives based on real problems and learners' prior knowledge, interests and experience.
Learners expect teachers to teach them what is required to pass a series of assessments.	The learner takes responsibility for their learning and actively seeks knowledge.
Learners reconstruct knowledge and information without really understanding it.	Learners construct knowledge by interacting with their teachers and the data gathered through different sources, with a view to solving the problem or task that has been given to them.
Learners sit in rows.	Learners work individually and in groups and often in front of computers which provide them with access to multiple resources.

Information is presented using PowerPoint, lectures, books and films.	The teacher acts as facilitator, helping learners to access and process information.

(This is adapted from EIC, 2004)

(ii) Kinaesthetic ('learning-by-doing')

A kinaesthetic learner is someone who learns best by doing, moving, touching, being involved in activities, coordinating, exploring and experiencing things first hand. They value making and learning from mistakes and creating a product or service. Kinaesthetic learners may find it difficult to engage in or learn from abstract examples or concepts.

Lecturers can adjust their session to take account of kinaesthetic learning preferences as follows:

- Providing physical demonstrations during a lecture or presentation (e.g. during a presentation on mobile phones, learners could be asked to demonstrate to their peers features they like using on their mobile phone)
- Video content can be included in PowerPoint presentations to make abstract examples or concepts more real.
- Provide visual aids, such as diagrams to demonstrate a point and ask learners to present their views about the content of the diagram to the rest of the group.
- Have more physical activities, e.g. using 'stick-it' notes to collect learner ideas and views, which they then attach to sheets on the classroom walls (this is a technique often used in professional training sessions). Once the exercise is completed other learners can wander around to read the comments on the 'stick-it' notes.
- Involve learners to demonstrate certain concepts (e.g. when discussing positive and negative body language, ask learners to adopt certain poses, such as crossing arms, looking away, etc.).

61

- Ask learners to add to or highlight points made on the white board / interactive white board or by using the wireless keyboard and mouse linked to the computer and data projector.

Even if learners do not have a preference for kinaesthetic learning, such activities can add variety to a session and increase engagement, although over-use could be counterproductive.

Kinaesthetic activities can be incorporated in virtually any topic, but some topics are more likely be a better fit. For instance, in staff selection role play can be used to demonstrate and assess interview techniques, while in ICT, a combination of role play and presentation could be used to deliver the benefits of a software solution to a client (which can also be a role played by a learner). These activities are likely to appeal to visual and auditory learners as well.

The main limitations with kinaesthetic learning are the degree of planning involved, learners' willingness to participate, managing several activities at once (it may work better with smaller groups), space constraints, especially if a lot of movement is required. Some subjects lend themselves to this type of learning (e.g. sport, music, science), while others are more traditional in approach, with fewer opportunities for its application (e.g. law, maths, economics).

(iii) Presentations

Strengths	Limitations
Experience of composing thoughts and ideas in a structured manner.	Requires support, guidance and motivation to plan and deliver an effective presentation.
Experience of speaking in front of a group, which is a transferrable skill.	Peers may not be receptive to the presentation; and if the

	topic is similar, very little new learning may take place.
Peer feedback is likely to keep learners engaged. It is also likely to provide learners delivering the presentation with an outline of a range of strengths and areas for development.	Learners need to be trained in providing constructive, effective and objective feedback to peers that are presenting.
Videoed presentations can be used for reflection in class and in the learner's own time, if they are provided with a copy.	Presentation skills are not normally assessed by awarding organisations, who are interested in the content delivered. This can reduce the importance attached to presentation technique. In the business world, presentation skills can sometimes be more important than the content, especially where it is part of a pitch – one among many that a client may have seen over the course of a day or week.
Learners whose first language is not English or who have poor written skills or who have dyslexia (and have support in place) are likely to benefit from delivering presentations, especially if these are before written assignments, since there are opportunities for instant peer and lecturer feedback, outlining strengths and areas for improvement; and the focus on structuring thoughts and ideas may benefit	Lecturers require a degree of experience, expertise and innovation in preparing learners for delivering effective presentations, especially with integration of multi-media content.

learners when completing written assignments.	
Group presentations provide an opportunity to share ideas, support and learn from each other and take risks.	There is a risk that one or more group members may under-contribute or not contribute at all in preparing the presentation, expecting others to complete their part of the work.

(iv) Role play

Strengths	Limitations
It provides an opportunity for learners to get a different point of view by placing themselves in the shoes of the role they are playing, thereby encouraging elements of sympathy and empathy.	Learners need to be willing to undertake the role play and require clear instructions of what is expected of them.
It should appeal to learners who have a preference for visual, auditory and kinaesthetic learning.	Lecturers need to provide an effective debriefing and bring together what the learner should have understood and learnt from undertaking the role play and to help them to reflect on the role play.
In some situations, learners can draw on their own previous experiences when undertaking the role play (e.g. when role playing customer service, learners will have had	Lecturers will need to carefully plan scenarios that are engaging, appeal to learners and have a direct relevance to the unit assessment criteria or session objectives, which can

experience of customer service as a customer and possibly as a sales assistant). This should increase engagement, motivation and confidence, leading to deeper understanding, relating prior experience to current learning.	be difficult within the time available. They also need to be carefully managed, which becomes more difficult with larger class sizes or classes with learners that are easily distracted.
Where learners are consulted and involved in designing the role play scenario, they are likely to have greater commitment to participating, especially if they want to play out a situation which they have seen, read or heard about or personally experienced.	Any improvisation or learner-led role play scenarios must be related to learning outcomes / assessment criteria and session objectives, which requires time, scrutiny and careful planning and management with other role play scenarios being allocated and coordinated.

3. The importance of providing opportunities for learners to develop their English, mathematics, ICT and other skills

(a) Achievement in learning

(i) Functional skills (English, maths and ICT)

Functional Skills are qualifications in English, maths and ICT, from Entry 1 to Level 2 that equip learners with the practical skills they need to live, learn and work successfully. They are suitable for learners of all ages and are a mandatory part of all apprenticeship frameworks[15] in England. Learners may already possess Level 2

---

[15] An apprenticeship framework is a definition of requirements for an apprenticeship programme, which is used by learning providers and employers to ensure that all apprenticeship programmes are delivered

qualifications (e.g. GCSEs) in English, maths and ICT, but learning providers, particularly those that are publicly funded are expected to actively find and take advantage of opportunities to embed / incorporate these elements into the course

(ii) Embedding functional skills across the subject

The embedding of English, maths and ICT discretely into topics and programmes is important in developing opportunities for progression and life and employability skills. In relation to progression, most further and higher education providers expect minimum standards of English and maths, while many employers also expect a minimum level of competence with using ICT. In fact, out of all three, English is probably the most important, since it provides the building blocks to accessing and interpreting various forms of information, including assessment and examination questions, even those relating to maths and science subjects. Ofsted also inspects the extent to which these elements are embedded into courses. Here are some examples of inspection comments from a range of subject areas:

"Wherever possible tutors integrate literacy and numeracy into assignments and they are vigilant in correcting misspellings in submitted work. Performing arts students are required to cost and budget planned productions to further their understanding of the financial aspects of the industry." (York; 01/2014)

"Teachers find very good opportunities to promote students' English and mathematics skills and develop their literacy and numeracy in most lessons. Students understand the importance and relevance of English and mathematics, both to their study programme and to their employment prospects." (10/2014)

---

consistently and to agreed standards. An apprentice is a trainee who combines practical training in a job with study, working alongside experienced staff, gaining job-specific skills, earning a wage and studying towards an apprenticeship qualification.

"Tuition in literacy and numeracy was a particularly effective and integral aspect of hairdressing and beauty therapy teaching and learning, which helped to improve learners' professional skills." (Ofsted; 03:2009)

"All apprentices are well aware of the importance of skills in English and mathematics and information and communication technology (ICT). They use these skills very well in their daily work to present a professional image." (11/2013)

"All staff reinforce the importance of English, mathematics and ICT skills well throughout each apprentice's programme. They identify spelling and punctuation errors in learners' work well and require apprentices to correct these in detailed progress reviews." (*Ibid.*)

"Apprentices pay due attention to using English, mathematics and ICT skills well to produce high-quality work." (*Ibid.*)

"On the very large majority of courses, teachers promote the importance of developing skills in English and, for the most part, mathematics, very well, both planning and seizing opportunities to contextualise their relevance very skilfully within the subject topic." (03/2014)

"Learners improve their literacy skills through a range of contextual activities. In one very good lesson, AS-level psychology learners produced highly imaginative mock tabloid newspaper articles on a psychological study. Science teachers insert deliberate spelling errors into their presentations in order that learners will identify them, and encourage learners to spell out technical terminology correctly." (*Ibid.*)

"Prompt actions taken by assessors are very successful in identifying the skills needs of apprentices. As a result, apprentices develop very good speaking, writing, mathematics and computing skills. For example, apprentices working at a car manufacturing company have embedded mathematics calibrations when calculating the balancing of wheels and monitor results through formulaic codes on an electronic database." (*Ibid.*)

(iii) Employability skills

Employability skills are skills that employers are likely to expect or desire from their prospective recruits. Based on a number of surveys undertaken in the UK, the table below shows the most important employability skills.[16] A third column has been added, which considers possible assessment methods or techniques that apply them and should assist in developing such skills in further education.

Skill	Characteristic	Assessment methods / techniques
Verbal communication	Ability to express one's ideas clearly and confidently in speech.	• Debates • Role play • Presentations • Discussions
Teamwork	Ability to work confidently within a group.	• Group work • Group presentations • Group research and projects
Commercial awareness	Understand the commercial factors affecting an organisation.	• Case studies • External visits • Work placements
Analysing and investigating	Problem solving. Ability to gather information in a systematic way in order to establish facts, trends or principles.	• Case studies • Reports • Research assignments
Initiative and self-motivation	Ability to act on initiative, identify opportunities and be proactive and proposing ideas and solutions.	• Simulations • Work roles (e.g. working with college clients, e.g. in a beauty salon or

---

[16] See further: http://www.kent.ac.uk/careers/sk/top-ten-skills.htm

		as part of a consultancy project) • Challenging role plays • Work-based assignments
Drive	Determination to get things done and looking for better ways of doing things.	• Completing challenging tasks / assignments which focus on evaluations and recommendations • Identifying and undertaking a research project / assignment
Written communication	Ability to express oneself effectively in writing.	• Report writing • Essays • Written responses, with supporting evidence
Planning and organising	Ability to plan and carry out activities effectively.	• Prepare and deliver: - a presentation - a report - a project
Flexibility	Ability to adapt to changing situations and environment.	• Being able to succeed in a range of assessment methods • Working with new team members • Managing own workload effectively (including resubmissions and retakes)
Time management	Effective time management and prioritising tasks in order to meet deadlines.	• Submit assignments on time. • Deliver presentations

		within a set time frame.
		• Attend sessions punctually.

(b) Personal skills

(i) Skills development / transferrable skills

Personal skills development and development of transferrable skills are important not just for work but also for life. As society, technology, working environments and working patterns change, so learners of all ages need to consider continually developing or expanding their range of skills. Naturally, the need for skills development is more immediate for children and those completing their secondary, further or university education and/or entering employment.

A range of personal and transferrable skills have been listed and briefly defined below.

Skill	Definition
Team work	Working effectively with a group of people to complete tasks / projects.
Written communication	Able to communicate ideas and information effectively in writing.
Spoken communication	Effective verbal communication of ideas.
Listening	Able to select important information when others are speaking and are seen to listen with care.

Logical argument	Able to put forward a point in a logical, ordered and concise manner.
Problem solving	Able to identify barriers to completion of tasks and devise solutions to overcome such barriers.
Analytical skills	Able to analyse and critically review and evaluate information.
Creativity	Able to create objects, systems or processes, using originality, imagination and inventiveness.
Flexibility	Able to adjust and adapt to changing situations.
Leadership	Able to get other people to work together or individually to accomplish a task / project.
Organisation	Able to structure or arrange resources and time to successfully complete a task or project.
Decision making	Able to make a calculated decision between two or more alternatives.
Numeracy	Able to work with and be selective about numerical data and undertake calculations.
Physical	Able to undertake physically demanding tasks.
Practical	Able to adopt a practical approach to solve problems.
Time management	Able to complete tasks within deadlines.

Multi-tasking	Able to undertake a range of tasks simultaneously or within a set timeframe.
Self confidence	Able to express ideas persuasively, diplomatically when working with a range of other people.
Commercial awareness	Is aware of and understands various internal and external factors affecting an organisation.
Self-development	Able to be self-critical about own performance and take action to improve or learn new things.
ICT	Able to use ICT to research, create, organise and present data.
Tact	Able to identify and manage sensitive situations, showing tact, diplomacy and honesty appropriately.
Critical thinking	Able to objectively analyse and evaluate an issue / matter in order to form a judgement.
Creative thinking	Able to think creatively by generating and exploring ideas and making original connections.
Independent enquiry	Able to evaluate information and undertake own investigations and planning what to do and how to go about it.
Empathy	Able to understand and share the feelings of another or at least give the appearance of doing so.

The above is not an exhaustive list and nor is it placed in order of importance. A learner would not be expected to work towards or be able to demonstrate all of the above skills. The cluster of skills that are essential to further study or employment depend on the subject, sector, position and organisational culture. For instance, a prospective barrister would be expected to be highly articulate, with excellent written and analytical skills, while a computer programmer working from home might need to be highly creative and analytical. Verbal and written skills would be less relevant.

Therefore, programmes should be planned, taking account of the skills needed for the subject, direct professional pathways to further study and employment and learner aspirations. These may not always be possible from the course content itself and could need a degree of innovation in teaching and learning, additional workshops or enrichment activities.

Ways to create an inclusive teaching and learning environment

1. The importance of creating an inclusive teaching and learning environment

(a) Valuing diversity

There are several arguments in favour of valuing and promoting diversity, not least of all the business case. We are living in an increasingly multi-cultural environment, where clients, customers and consumers come in many shapes, sizes and ages, from different faiths, racial backgrounds, nationalities and varying sexual orientation. Competition for jobs, clients, customers and consumers is increasing. Geography is less of a barrier to commerce and learning, with the growth of online platforms and flexible solutions. Consequently, ignoring diversity can have adverse financial consequences, such as lost sales or missed opportunities. Certainly, there are racial and religious tensions and it is unlikely that these will ever disappear. In fact they may increase, with the impact of globalisation and 'blow-back'[17] / retaliation from wars in other countries.

Lecturers, therefore, need to be sensitive to tensions between different groups of individuals and find ways to manage and reduce such tensions in the educational environment. Some of these tensions may be based on stereotypes, misconceptions, unjustified prejudice or misunderstanding or lack of knowledge or understanding. One way to alleviate some of these is through structured 'ice-breakers' during induction, where learners introduce themselves and provide some background or interesting facts about their culture, religion or personal experiences relating to equality and diversity (positive and negative experiences) and how they expect others to treat them. The learning provider's policies and procedures can also be introduced during induction to outline equality and diversity related expectations the organisation has of its learners and what learners can expect from the organisation.

Cultural and religious celebrations, particularly where food and music is involved tend to work well if managed effectively. In terms of disability, learning difficulties, medical conditions and different learning styles and ability ranges, lecturers need to take these into account when planning their teaching, learning and assessment strategies.

If reasonable adjustments are not made and different learner needs not considered, it could lead to poor learner performance during assessments and/or learners leaving the programme or not completing it successfully. This has financial and social consequences. Financial consequences include loss of revenue, especially if the learning provider receives government funding per

---

[17] This is an unforeseen and unwanted effect, result, or set of repercussions.

learner and is paid in instalments while the learner remains on the programme, together with an element/percentage for successful completion of the programme. Where government funding is not provided, learners may be paying in instalments themselves. If they leave the programme early, the learning provider may lose the remaining instalment payments. If they remain on the programme, but do not make satisfactory progress, they may not be able to continue on to a higher programme with the learning provider, which again leads to a loss of revenue. In addition, poor performance and/or early withdrawal from a programme could be counterproductive to the learners' group dynamic, its morale and motivation.

There are education and career-related benefits to diversity for learners. These can include the following:

- an opportunity to share different perspectives and life experiences
- the quality of decision-making (including personal, career-related or educational) may be enhanced. For instance, a mature learner might have worked in different fields that other learners intend to enter, so they can discuss industry practice and expectations with them;
- being aware of and sensitive to a range of cultures, backgrounds, ages, sexual orientation, faith and disability increases a learner's ability to adapt to working with different people in various environments and contexts. It should also develop a degree of empathy and tolerance, which can be used in other contexts. Empathy is becoming increasingly important for managers in many business sectors;[18]
- the Equality Act 2010 and corporate social responsibility and diversity agendas at many large organisations place high expectations of their staff in relation to equality and diversity. Becoming familiar with the requirements

---

[18] See for instance:
http://www.ccl.org/Leadership/pdf/research/EmpathyInTheWorkplace.pdf

75

and expectations during the education and training stage should provide a good basis for dealing with these aspects effectively during employment.

(b) Challenging discriminatory and anti-social behaviours

Lecturers are normally expected to challenge discrimination and anti-social behaviour in their sessions or when supervising learners and report such instances accordingly to their line manager. Follow-up action should then ensue promptly where discriminatory conduct or anti-social behaviour is proven. This can take the form of disciplinary proceedings against the learner. In some cases, a verbal intervention by the lecturer to halt a discussion becoming prejudiced, offensive or discriminatory may be sufficient to remind learners about the boundaries of acceptable conduct. Where minor infractions are not challenged, they could lead to major issues over time.

(c) Encouraging peer support

Group work and peer assessment provide opportunities to develop informal peer support structures. More formal support mechanisms can include peer mentoring, where one learner mentors and officially supports another. In such instances, peer mentors require some training and need to be clear about the scope and remit of their role. If organised and managed effectively, there are benefits to mentors and mentees. For instance, mentors can re-enforce their existing learning when guiding their mentees, they can improve their communication and leadership skills, while mentees are likely to feel less inhibited to discuss concerns about their programme and topics they find challenging with their mentors, and it provides additional support to assist them to master their subject. Peer mentoring seems to work particularly well when the mentor is at a more advanced stage of the programme and is therefore in a better position to reflect and guide the mentee.

Some learning providers may also have ex-students as mentors or guest speakers. This is likely to have a significant impact on existing learners, since the ex-students can empathise with them and discuss strategies they found useful in completing the programme and assess how relevant the skills gained from the programme are to current employment practices. Such advice, guidance and affirmation should increase learner morale and motivation, potentially reducing some of the barriers they may have had, such as lack of access to current information about external progression routes and career paths in practice.

(d) Minimising barriers to learning

Barriers to learning are any factors that prevent or reduce a learner's ability to learn. Such barriers may be physical (e.g. ability to travel to the learning provider due to poor transport links or due to a physical impairment), personal (e.g. family commitments, such as looking after children), financial (e.g. ability to pay for the programme or related learning resources), language-related (e.g. English may be an additional language and not adequate for all elements of the programme), related to learning difficulties (e.g. dyslexia), psychological (e.g. a bad experience of education and training in the past) or pedagogical (e.g. learner may have been out of formal education for a long time).

A lecturer is not expected to identify or adapt to all of these barriers to learning, most of which are outside of their remit. However, being aware of individual needs and barriers to learning should allow a more considered and flexible approach to be adopted. Here are some examples of simple strategies to reduce barriers to learning.

Barrier to learning	Possible strategy	Likely outcome
Unable to attend on time, due to poor transport facilities	Consider enrolling in a class which has a later start time.	Learner has more time to reach the class.
Physical impairment	Identify the impact on learning, and reasonable adjustments that can be made. Seek permission for the adjustment internally and from the awarding organisation, where necessary.	Learner is able to complete the programme and assessments without their disability disadvantaging their achievement.
Unable to purchase learning resources.	Refer learner to student finance department, which may be able to provide some financial assistance with acquiring learning resources (e.g. there may be a student hardship fund).	Learner is not disadvantaged due to financial constraints.
Family commitments	Discuss possible absences and arrange catch-up sessions or provide learning materials for the sessions that will be missed.	Learners do not fall behind and are able to catch-up more easily.
Language related	Liaise with English / ESOL staff to arrange additional English workshops.	By attending additional English workshops, learners improve their standard of English.
Dyslexia	Make reasonable adjustments to assessments, use more visual content in sessions and alter feedback format and method.	Learners are able to engage more effectively with the materials, assessments and sessions.

Bad prior experience with education	Consult learners about individual learning styles, preferences and past experiences. These can inform differentiation strategies, providing more individual support and guidance to learners with bad previous education experience.	Learners have a more positive experience of education and therefore should have improved morale and motivation.
Out of formal education for several years	Extended induction sessions are provided and on-going additional drop-in workshops to ease learners back to formal educational requirements.	Learners increase engagement in lessons, with assessments and perform well on the programme after a period of adjustment and possible initial under-performance as a result.

2. The importance of selecting teaching and learning approaches, resources and assessment methods to meet individual learner needs

(a) Alignment to meet learner's knowledge and skills requirements

Learners are likely to have different starting points, based on previous learning, qualifications and experience. Awarding organisations require learning providers to recognise prior certificated and/or experiential learning (i.e. to apply to them for partial or full exemption from some qualification units where the prior learning is directly relevant to the assessment criteria). In practice, recognition of prior learning is seldom applied formally.

Where learners have relevant prior experience of a topic, lecturers can involve them in the discussion and ask them to contribute their experiences and understanding. In sessions where learners have relevant management experience, discussion, analysis and case studies relating to management can draw on such experiences and be adapted to be more practical, advanced / challenging.

Learners may have different aspirations and motivation to undertake the programme. For instance, some learners may require the qualification for entry to further study or employment, while some others may want to improve or extend their existing knowledge and skills set and others may be taking the programme for pleasure. Where gaining the qualification is the primary motive, lecturers may spend more time focusing on assessment / examination technique. Where, however, learners are more interested in gaining the skills rather than the qualification, then lecturers could spend more time on developing and extending those skills and focusing less on assessment and examination technique. Lecturers need to be sensitive to individual motives for undertaking the programme and differentiate accordingly, providing instruction, delivery and resources that meet each learner's needs or at least be able to guide them to additional reading or resources.

(b) Alignment to assessment requirements and schedule (balancing competing priorities)

Lecturers often need to balance the needs of learners with awarding organisation regulations. These can include strict protocols for assessment schedules (i.e. timeframe for assessments), formative and summative assessments, resubmission timeframes and frequency and type of feedback. However, lecturers still have a degree of discretion as to the assessment methods used and the teaching and learning strategies applied. Even centre devised assignment briefs need to meet strict awarding organisation requirements. For instance, assignment briefs for a leading UK awarding organisation cannot have detailed guidance on how to complete the assignment. Sometimes it is a delicate balancing act, especially with internal assessments and related quality assurance.

(c) Responsive to group demographic and dynamic

Teaching, learning and assessment strategies should be aligned as far as possible to learner profiles, preferences, aspirations, interests and expectations and differentiated accordingly. This works particularly well when delivering training to clients, who may have their own requirements and negotiate how the purchased programme is to be delivered within awarding organisation constraints.

(d) Actively engaging learners in the learning process

Learner engagement in learning, sometimes known as 'learner voice'[19] or 'student engagement'[20], involves meetings, surveys and evaluative feedback from learners about teaching, learning, assessment and aspects of quality assurance and even consulting and involving learners in finalising, implementing and reviewing plans, policies and procedures that relate to them and their learning. Such involvement and feedback allows learning providers to align and calibrate their teaching, learning, assessment, quality assurance and quality improvement and enhancement strategies to meet learners' needs and create a positive learner/student experience.

---

[19] See further: *LEARNER ENGAGEMENT: A review of learner voice initiatives across the UK's education sectors*, Futurelab

[20] See further: http://www.qaa.ac.uk/partners/students/student-engagement-at-qaa and *Chapter B5* ("Student Engagement") of the UK Quality Code for Higher Education.

Learner engagement also acts as a form of check and balance on the learning provider, assuming that senior management at the learning provider is receptive to constructive critique (i.e. learner views and scheduled meetings with senior management may highlight emerging or existing issues at programme and department level, which could otherwise not be apparent to senior management). Receiving and responding to learner feedback and views[21] in the form of programme improvements and enhancements should increase learner satisfaction and retention and achievement, which in turn has positive financial implications from a government funding perspective and private funding position (see earlier discussion above). Inspection and review bodies examine the extent to which learner engagement takes place, with Ofsted considering the 'learner voice' and QAA considering 'student engagement'. This holds learning providers to account in various respects (at least those that are inspected and reviewed by external bodies).

Potential benefits of learner engagement:

- learners have a greater sense of ownership over their learning
- increased learner motivation
- learners have improved self-esteem
- greater achievement
- improved relationships with peers and lecturers
- increased self-efficacy (i.e. the extent of belief in one's own ability to complete tasks and achieve goals)
- greater transparency of organisational processes
- increased responsiveness to emerging and existing issues at programme and department level
- increased patience with various quality assurance processes, such as standardisation, double marking, internal verification, external verification).

---

[21] These tend to be through a system of learner representatives / class representatives, who meet with middle or senior management on a scheduled basis.

Potential risks of not including or responding to learner engagement:

- learner disengagement and disillusionment with their educational experience
- reduced participation and engagement levels, since learners may not feel 'listened to'
- fewer recommendations to peers about studying at the learning provider.

In most learning providers, learner engagement, in its many guises, informs annual monitoring and review and quality assurance and improvement processes. These formal processes then form part of department and organisational level self-assessments and quality improvement plans or equivalent self-evaluation documents and action plans. It can therefore be said that active learner engagement and a genuine commitment to it should contribute to a learning provider's efforts for continuous quality improvement and enhancement.

(e) Responding to individual learning needs

Adjusting delivery methods / strategies

Learning difficulty, disability or medical condition	Key challenges	Possible adjustments to delivery
Dyslexia	Processing auditory information.	Ensure that overall discussion allows for reiteration, clarification of new terms and regular pauses for reflection and to catch up.

	Developing reliable short term memory and recall.	Reduce overall delivery speed.
	Sequencing information.	Supply handouts and explanatory lists of new concepts and unfamiliar terms.
	Multi-tasking (especially note taking).	Encourage students to audio record instruction and to audio record sessions
	Processing information under time constraints.	Supplement verbal information with written or e-learning versions as introductions, summaries and *aide mémoires*. Arrange study skills sessions on taking accurate notes (funded through the Disabled Students' Allowances scheme).
Asthma	Student has weeklong absences.	Ensure that lectures and seminars are supported with good quality handouts and electronic versions.
Diabetes	Students may be working under par or missing sessions due to diabetic episodes.	Provide good quality notes to cover student absence.
Epilepsy	Photosensitive epilepsy may be triggered by natural or artificial flashing or flickering lights.	Avoid displaying visual material that contains flickering or repetitive patterns.

(adapted from Waterfield *et. al.* 2006)

Adjusting assessment methods / strategies

Learning difficulty, disability or medical condition	Assessment method	Key challenges	Possible adjustments
Dyslexia	Written	Taking longer to achieve the objectives of written tasks with deadlines.	Provide early notification of assignment cut-off dates and flexible deadlines.
	Written	Stress induced by deadlines leading to poor performance.	Explore the possibilities of alternatives to written, assessed tasks.
	Group work	Increased anxiety caused by group work.	Devise and disseminate clear written briefings for all students on the interpersonal dimensions of group work.
	Presentation	Problems with verbal fluency, processing language and saying the wrong thing.	Offer support to practice presentation skills and timing. Explore the possibilities of alternatives to presentations.
	Examination	Legibly writing at speed.	Use of a PC. Assistive technologies such as text-to-speech and mind mapping software
Asthma	Group work	Medication affects the student's	Consider the implications

| | | stamina and sleep patterns. | when organising group work tasks.

Allow additional time to achieve tasks and be flexible with deadlines. |
| Epilepsy | Any | Students who have seizures are likely to under perform for several days either side of the seizure. | Consider alternative assessment activities and flexible assessment timetables. |

(adapted from Waterfield *et. al.* 2006)

Adjusting feedback to learners

Learning difficulty	Key challenges	Possible adjustments to feedback
Dyslexia	Processing auditory information.	Verbal feedback supported by written feedback (see below)
	Accurately comprehending written material.	When giving written feedback, use bullet points and summarise rather than using dense pros.

(adapted from Waterfield *et. al.* 2006)

Adjusting learning resources

Learning difficulty	Key challenges	Possible adjustments to learning resources
Dyslexia	Accurately comprehending written material.	Specialist terms need explaining through word lists and glossaries.

	Reading accurately at a competent rate.	Avoid too much underlining, capitals and italics.
		Simplify dense blocks of text.
		Use bullet points.
		Leave wide spaces.
		Left-justify text.
		Make documents available electronically so that students can modify them to meet their needs and to read at their own pace.

(adapted from Waterfield *et. al.* 2006)

3. Ways to engage and motivate learners

(a) Active, clear and shared outcomes

Involve learners in discussing, understanding and internalising assessment tasks and criteria. Showing exemplar materials (i.e. examples of similar completed learner work) should make it easier for learners to comprehend what is required / expected of them. Lecturers can also suggest possible approaches that learners can take with tasks.

(b) Individual, paired and group activities

Individual working should increase independence and a sense of achievement, while paired and group working should introduce a social and fun element, but all group members need to be clear about their duties and responsibilities to each other and ensure the work is shared equally.

(c) Encouraging creative and critical thinking

These are important life skill and useful transferrable skills for further study and employment. Additional time may need to be set aside in sessions or embedded in the timetable to undertake skills development and tasks that encourage critical and creative thinking, including problem-solving activities.

(d) Using a range of teaching and learning approaches

Learners are likely to respond positively (after a period of adjustment) to varied teaching and learning approaches (see examples already examined earlier).

(e) Meeting appropriate targets

Target setting and their regular monitoring and review are important in ensuring that learners are progressing in a timely and appropriate manner relative to their starting point and potential. Such target setting and monitoring is normally done through individual learning plans.

(f) Learners' involvement in their assessment

Involving learners in selecting some of the assessment methods or case study content is likely to encourage 'buy-in' / commitment to the assessment, especially if they understand that the methods will benefit them in developing transferrable skills for further study and employment.

(g) Providing positive, constructive feedback that is responsive to individual needs

Learners may require feedback in a range of formats, depending on disability, learning difficulty or medical condition. Learners are likely to benefit from a combination of written and verbal feedback, with opportunities to ask questions and clarify the feedback provided. Feedback should be constructive, fair, detailed, developmental and have positive elements and clearly identify areas for improvement, with actions / steps needed to achieve such improvements.

4. Ways to establish ground rules with learners

(a) Student participation and ownership

Ground rules can be established at the beginning of a programme, unit, assignment, session or even before an activity is undertaken. Ground rules can include the expectations or requirements and standards of conduct or learning outcomes that need to be followed or achieved. In many cases, ground rules need to be made explicit either verbally or in writing and repeated from time to time as a reminder. However, the adherence to and effectiveness of ground rules depend on learner 'buy-in' / ownership. Where learners have been consulted and involved in negotiating ground rules, they are more likely to take ownership over them and enforce them within their group and peers.

(b) Negotiating behaviour and learning

What is acceptable behaviour depends on context, the activity and the subject matter. For instance, in a role play requiring a learner to act-out being a rude customer, some misbehaviour is necessary. The conduct expected in a class, with active group work activities, may be very different from the conduct expected when visiting a professional work place or court room. Learners will need explicit ground rules as to what is generally acceptable and in different contexts, especially if the context or situation is new to them. A degree of negotiation may be necessary to obtain commitment. Discussing and agreeing teaching, learning and assessment methods and strategies should also increase learner commitment and motivation. However, the degree of negotiation that takes place will vary depending on the nature and background of a group. For instance, mature professional learners (e.g. middle managers) may well expect to be offered different options of or variations to the teaching, learning and assessment on their programme, particularly where it is customised to their particular needs (e.g. purchased by their employer). There is likely to be less flexibility with programmes for 16-18 year-olds, who may have limited experience of different teaching, learning and assessment strategies, although even with this group the choice and frequency of role play, presentations, external visits and work placements can be negotiated to meet their preferred learning styles and interests.

(c) Exploring diversity

Discussing differences in social, cultural, religious, racial and sexual orientation and relating these to their subject area, future employment contexts and what employers expect should provide a rationale for behaviour that is non-discriminatory and progressive. The difficulties, however, remain of balancing tensions between some of the protected characteristics, such as sexual orientation and faith. These topics need to be handled with care and diplomacy.

(d) Understanding and demonstrating mutual respect and
   acceptable social behaviours

In addition to the above approaches, learners should be made aware of the learning provider's policies, procedures, disciplinary steps and likely outcomes if there is a lack of mutual respect and anti-social behaviour occurs. Any such behaviour needs to be challenged promptly in order to stem any escalation.

Micro-teach

Planning inclusive teaching and learning

1. Inclusive teaching and learning plan

(a) Planning the session

Planning for a micro-teach session is important both in terms of passing the assessment, but also ensuring that the session goes smoothly. An important starting point is to select a topic of personal interest or in which the person delivering the session is knowledgeable. In order to maximise learner engagement, learners should be consulted as to their preference of topics for the micro-teach or at least their learning styles, content preferences and assessment activities. A lesson plan must normally be completed. There are five important sections to this: (i) the aims and session objectives and linking these to assessment objectives and strategies, (ii) a crisp introduction that outlines the session objectives and what will be covered in the session, (iii) content delivery, with teaching and learning activities, resources to be used, assessment strategies and differentiation, (iv) closing the session, with checks on the extent to which the session objectives have been met, and (v) post-session evaluation of the extent to which the lesson plan was effective in practice.

(b) Identifying individual learning styles

It is useful to consult learners and ask them to complete a VARK questionnaire to identify their preferred learning styles. This can then inform the content and style of delivery and assessments used. Ideally, a range of learning styles should be used and there are likely to be some resource and time constraints which limit the extent to which the full range of learning styles can be used. It also depends on the nature of the subject covered in the micro-teach. For instance, learning to use a DSLR camera may require more visual and kinaesthetic activity, while a session on History may have more visual and auditory elements. Both sessions could have some read and write activities during assessment of learning (e.g. using multiple choice or short answer questions at the end to confirm what learning has taken place).

(c) Identifying prior knowledge and experience of the proposed
   micro-teach activity

Identifying learners' prior knowledge and experience of the proposed micro-teach session will be important for planning teaching, learning, assessment and differentiation strategies. One of the aims of the micro-teach is to demonstrate that new learning is taking place. If, for instance, a micro-teach is delivered that introduces Spanish nouns and verbs to learners that are native Spanish speakers, there is likely to be very limited new learning taking place. A topic should be selected that provides opportunities for new learning to take place. If learner knowledge and experience of the topic is at different levels, it creates challenges, but also provides good opportunities for using differentiation (which requires a lot of planning and effective delivery). However, a good lesson is one that is differentiated effectively and takes account of all learning needs.

(d) Involving learners in the selection of the micro-teach topic

If the session is to be delivered to peers or colleagues who are also delivering a micro-teach, then the topic should be one that is of mutual interest, since this is likely to increase learner engagement. For instance, a session on cooking tips for a particular dish, with a sample of the finished product that the learners can taste and comment on, adds to an interesting experience, increased motivation and engagement, especially if the tasting is linked to an element of learning (e.g. the impact on presentation and taste of adding saffron to rice or green chillies to a curry dish). The assessment can then be a combination of written and verbal assessments before and after tasting the dish. If some learners have dietary restrictions and these are not considered at the planning stage of the micro-teach and when preparing the dish, then learners will not fully engage / participate in the session; this could in turn adversely impact on the assessment and inclusive learning.[22]

2. Selection of teaching and learning approaches, resources and assessment methods in relation to meeting individual learner needs

(a) Individual or paired / group activities?

Paired and group activity provide a good opportunity to encourage peer discussion, more active learner engagement and a greater focus on being learner-centred. It can also be used to for peer

---

[22] The example used here involves the following: the candidate delivering the micro-teach has already prepared and brought in the dish. The micro-teach uses a range of visual aids to discuss certain preparatory steps. Learners are then assessed on what they have been taught. They are presented with the dish, which they taste and are asked some further questions to check their learning. (Learners should be questioned about possible allergies and dietary requirements at the planning stage for health and safety reasons.)

assessment of learning (e.g. swapping and marking each other's exercises at the end of the micro-teach). However, learners need to be comfortable and familiar with paired / group activity and how to contribute accordingly.

(b) Teacher or learner-centred approach?

Most sessions will have elements of teacher and learner-centred approaches. However, a good session will be more learner-centred, actively involving learners in their learning, checking their learning, encouraging participation, engagement and discussions, questions, as well as paired and group activities. The balance should be more towards learner-centred than teacher-centred approaches.

(c) Application of VARK

Using multi-media elements in a PowerPoint provides opportunities to appeal to visual, auditory, read and kinaesthetic elements, while written exercises cover the remaining 'write' element of VARK. It is therefore relatively easy to cover all aspects of VARK. It is then a question of the weighting or importance given to each of these elements. This is likely to be informed by learner stated preferences, the subject content, resourcing and time constraints.

(d) Resources

When considering the appropriateness and fitness for purpose of resources, a number of aspects need to be considered, including prior subject knowledge, experience, learning style preferences, cultural and religious sensitivities, disability and learning difficulties. Resources then need to be sourced, developed or adapted accordingly.

(e) Assessment

The choice of methods and techniques will depend on learner profiles, background knowledge, experience and preferences, as well as time and resource constraints. For instance, a session demonstrating the features of a new mobile phone may require learners to display that they have learnt how to use these features by using the mobile phone as part of the assessment. However, if there is only one model of the phone available then the assessment part of the micro-teach will need to take account of this, whereas ideally if each person had simultaneous access to the device more checking of learning could take place in the shorter time frame.

Delivering inclusive teaching and learning

1. Applying teaching and learning approaches, resources, and assessment methods to meet individual learner needs

(a) Using a lesson plan

The delivery of the session and related activities and assessments should match the lesson plan. After all, in a lesson observation a lecturer is assessed on their preparation for the session and the extent to which they have delivered in line with the lesson plan. In some cases an experienced lecturer might deviate from the lesson plan and improvise, especially if learners are engaging more effectively than anticipated and a group activity requires more time or further elements in order to maximise learning. This could be justified from a learner-centred perspective, but is a high risk strategy for a person with limited teaching experience delivering a micro-teach.

(b) Factors to consider

- learner qualifications, experience and interests in the topic to be delivered at the lesson planning stage and ensuring this is followed through during the delivery
- whether learners are on-task and fully engaged during the micro-teach (if not, then corrective action may be required, such as directed questions or gaining their attention)
- the timing of the delivery activity or assessment may not be as planned. Slight under or over-runs are less of an issue. In order to avoid under-runs, additional activities could be planned to accommodate such a situation (e.g. additional exercises or extended discussion or group activity).

2. Communication methods that meet individual learner needs

(a) Language register and intonation

The standard or level of language needs to be in line with what learners can understand. Complex or technical terms, if required, should be explained and/or included in a glossary (see the glossary section of this book for an example). Register (i.e. a particular style of speaking or writing) and intonation (i.e. variation of spoken pitch) are also important. For instance, in relation to register, the style of language used in law is quite distinct from medicine and distinct again from ICT. The style needs to be adapted according to the audience's knowledge and experience. For instance, the register used for a medically qualified audience is likely to be much higher and more complex (presupposing a lot of medical experience and technical knowledge) than that used for A level Biology students.

Intonation provides variety and stimulates attention. Imagine if a lecturer adopted a monotone approach, with little or no change in vocal pitch. It is likely to be a boring session, even though the content may be sound. A good example of a boring, monotone delivery can be found at the following You Tube link:

https://www.youtube.com/watch?v=9Q-9NMTRigl Contrast this
with the following video by the late Steve Jobs, speaking in 2005:
https://www.youtube.com/watch?v=D1R-jKKp3NA The latter has an
interesting story, suitable pauses and changes in pace and pitch.
This adds emotional content, variation and retains audience
attention.

(b) Body language

Body language should be positive, being culturally sensitive, yet
engaging, maintaining eye contact (within reason), facing all
learners (as opposed to one section of learners), not crossing arms
or facing away from the audience to reading off the PowerPoint for
long periods at a time. Some arm movement is important for
emphasis, so long as it is not distracting or excessive.

(c) Inclusive questioning

All learners must be engaged in a session for it to be effective. This
can be achieved by a mix of undirected and directed questions,
group work, a range of activities and talking to each learner during
group activities to check learning. Questions should be
differentiated, with levels of difficulty based on learner knowledge,
experience and aptitude for the topic or subject. Where learners do
not understand a question, rephrasing it and asking it in a different
way, with simpler examples may be an effective technique to elicit
the desired response and engage and motivate the learner.
Sometimes learners know the answer, but do not understand the
question because of the way it is phrased.

3. Constructive feedback that meets individual learner needs

(a) Identifying opportunities to provide feedback in own and others' micro-teach

Constructive, supportive and timely feedback are important in any teaching and learning session. There are three main opportunities to provide such feedback. The first is during question and answers, where learners are praised for a good response and given guidance where a response does not quite meet expectations or could be better; the second is when checking learning during assessments, and the third is when giving peer feedback to others delivering a micro-teach (at the end of their micro-tech session).

(b) Types of feedback

Constructive feedback normally includes elements of summative and formative feedback. It usually considers and praises the strong elements of a response or assessment. This is typically followed by actions the learner could take to improve their response or, where the response is good, how it can be enhanced / made even better.

Summative feedback arrives at a judgement, grade or mark. Effective summative feedback would normally be detailed, outlining how and why a response met the assessment criteria or question or how and why it did not do so. Formative feedback usually examines two aspects: improvement and enhancement. Improvement seeks to identify gaps or errors in a response and advises the learner on the steps they can take to overcome these and improve their response. Enhancement looks at a response that is already good and advises on how the response could be even better (it is seeking excellence and 'stretch').

Evaluating delivery of inclusive teaching and learning

1. Reviewing the effectiveness of own delivery of inclusive teaching and learning

(a) Questions to consider

- What were the strengths or what worked particularly well during the planning and delivery stages?
- Were there weaknesses or missed opportunities during planning and delivery? And if so, what would I do differently next time I deliver this session?
- Are there gaps in my knowledge, training planning or delivery abilities? If so, what steps can I take to remedy / strengthen these?
- Were there areas of good practice? Were these peculiar to this group of learners or could they be replicated with other learners (and would any adjustments be needed)? How can this good practice be maintained?
- What can I learn from the feedback from my peers?
- Are there any techniques I could incorporate from those I have seen during the micro-teach delivered by my peers?

(b) Using AET tutor and group/peer feedback

- Tutor and learner / group /peer feedback should inform the evaluation of own micro-teach, together with own evaluation.
- If there is a second opportunity to deliver a micro-teach, it would be useful to receive feedback from the AET tutor and peers to evaluate the extent to which the second micro-teach was better than the first.

2. Identifying areas for self-improvement and development in delivery of inclusive teaching and learning

(a) Identifying areas for improvement based on self-assessment, lesson plan and group/peer feedback

If the micro-teach session has been videoed, then the video together with the following should be used as part of the evaluation and reflection process:

- a critical evaluation and review of the lesson plan and the extent to which it was followed in the delivery
- a review of the micro-teach video, examining own delivery and learner response and engagement
- AET tutor written and verbal feedback
- peer feedback at the end of the micro-teach (assuming it has been recorded / noted)
- critical reflection on own performance when compared with that of peers and those in practice (if the candidate has personally observed an experienced lecturer / trainer).

References

EIC (Education Initiative Centre) (2004): *What is Student Centred Learning?*, University of
Westminster

Ofsted	(10/2014)	*Strode College*, Ofsted inspection report, inspection number 446539, URN: 130806
	(03/2014)	*Chichester College*, Ofsted inspection report, inspection number 429157, URN: 130843
	(01/2014):	*York College*, Ofsted inspection report, inspection number 423353, URN: 130594
	(01/2014b)	*Queen Elizabeth Academy Trust*, Ofsted inspection report, inspection number 431076
	(11/2013)	*QA Ltd*, Ofsted inspection report, inspection number 423793, URN: 54022
	(09/2011)	*Ashton Sixth Form College*, Ofsted inspection report, inspection number 376179, URN: 130518
	(11/2009)	*Loreto College*, Ofsted inspection report, inspection number 342775, URN: 130503
	(03/2009)	*Identifying good practice: a survey of college provision in hairdressing and beauty therapy*
	(01/2008)	*Identifying good practice: a survey of business, administration and law in colleges*

Waterfield, J, West, B, Chalkley, B (2006): *Developing an inclusive curriculum for students with dyslexia and hidden disabilities*, University of Plymouth

Command verbs (used in this unit)

COMMAND VERB	DEFINITION
Communicate	Convey or exchange spoken or written information
Compare	Examine the subjects in detail looking at similarities and differences
Describe	Provide an extended range of detailed factual information about the topic or item in a logical way.
Devise	Plan or invent (a complex procedure, system or mechanism) by careful thought
Explain	Make something clear to someone by describing or revealing relevant information in more detail.
Identify	Ascertain the origin, nature, or definitive characteristics of
Justify	Give a comprehensive explanation of the reasons for actions and/or decisions
Provide	Identify and give relevant and detailed information in relation to the subject
Review	Revisit and consider the merit of analysing the positive and negative aspects
Summarise	Give the main ideas or facts in a concise way.
Use	Apply

Glossary of key terms used in this textbook

TERM	DEFINITION
Access arrangement	Adjustments to examinations.
Accreditation of prior learning (APL)	APL is the generic term for the accreditation of prior learning, whether the result of a formal course or learning through experience. (APL is the term normally used by awarding bodies, such as universities. The equivalent used by awarding organisations is RPL.)
Accreditation of prior certificated learning (APCL)	APCL is based on certified (or certificated) learning following a formal course of study at another learning provider or institute. (APCL is the term normally used by awarding bodies, such as universities.)
Accreditation of prior experiential learning (APEL)	APEL is based on experiential learning - learning achieved through experience, rather than on a formal course of study. (APEL is the term normally used by awarding bodies, such as universities.)
Andragogy / Andragogical	These are the methods and practices used in teaching adults, focusing on independent, self-directed and/or cooperative learning, where adults exercise control over much of their learning experience, with grades being less important to them than gaining knowledge and skills.
Annual monitoring and review (AMR)	"Annual Monitoring and Review involves reflection on the effectiveness and viability of programmes, drawing on consultation with students and consideration of a range of inputs, including external examiners' reports, internal and external student survey outcomes, and other qualitative and quantitative information. The aim is to highlight and record those areas of provision that have gone well over the previous year and to highlight those in

	which the need for improvement, to further enhance the student experience, has been identified." http://www.ncl.ac.uk/quilt/assets/documents/qsh-amr-policy.pdf
Assessment criteria	Each learning outcome contains assessment criteria that are used to assess the learner evidence submitted. These are normally related to grades.
Assessor	This refers to the person responsible for making decisions about whether learners' work achieves the national standard required for certification (e.g. whether assessment criteria and any related grade descriptors have been met).
Awarding organisation	Although the terms awarding organisation and awarding body have been used to mean the same thing, awarding organisations are normally regulated by Ofqual and do not possess degree awarding powers.
Awarding body	Although the terms awarding body and awarding organisation have been used to mean the same thing, an awarding body is normally an organisation with degree awarding powers, such as a university.
Command verb	This is a verb that requires a specific action and is normally placed at the beginning of an assessment criteria, such as 'outline', 'describe', 'explain', 'analyse', 'evaluate'.
Diagnostic assessment	This is an assessment used to discover a candidate's strengths and weaknesses. It is often used to assess a learner's literacy, numeracy, ICT or subject specific skills or knowledge.
Differentiation	This can be viewed as the process by which differences between learners are accommodated so that all students in a group have the best possible chance of learning. It can be divided into 7

	categories, including differentiation by **task** (different tasks or exercises for different ability ranges), by **grouping** (mixed-ability groups), by **resources** (varying resources according to learner needs and abilities, such as providing basic resources and complex/advanced resources), by **pace** (learners working at a different pace can be given support or more challenging activities, so that whether a learner is falling behind, keeping up or completing exercises early in a session, support and extension materials ensure that all learners maintain momentum), by **outcome** (all students undertake the same task, but a range of results / grades are expected and considered as acceptable), by **dialogue and support** (identifying which learners need detailed explanations in simple language and which learners can engage in dialogue at a more sophisticated level. The teacher may also use directed questioning to produce a range of responses and use difficult follow-up questions to challenge the more able learners), and by **assessment** (learners are assessed on an on-going basis so that teaching, and the other methods of differentiation, can be continuously adjusted according to the learners' needs).
Diversity	There is no fixed or legal definition for diversity. It can be viewed as recognising and celebrating difference.
Equality	"Equality is about ensuring that every individual has an equal opportunity to make the most of their lives and talents, and believing that no one should have poorer life chances because of where, what or whom they were born, what they

	believe, or whether they have a disability." http://www.equalityhumanrights.com/private-and-public-sector-guidance/education-providers/secondary-education-resources/useful-information/understanding-equality
External Examiner (EE)	An external examiner is a person from another awarding body or awarding organisation, who monitors the assessment, moderation, double marking, standardisation and internal verification process of a learning provider for fairness, academic standards and quality assurance.
External moderation	An external moderator ensures that a learning provider is continuing to meet an awarding organisation's academic and quality standards by reassessing candidate's work. This normally applies to coursework.
External Verifier (EV)	An external verifier is appointed by an awarding organisation to ensure that the learning provider's / centre's own quality assurance systems are being implemented effectively in order to maintain national standards by <ul><li>providing information, advice and support to centres</li><li>certifying delivery/assessment practice and centre procedures (e.g. ensuring that assessment decisions are consistent with national standards)</li><li>maintaining records of visits and providing feedback (including essential actions, recommendations and areas of good practice)</li></ul>

Ibid.	This is the term used to provide an endnote / footnote / citation or reference for a source that was cited in the preceding endnote / footnote or reference.
Inclusive learning	This is about ensuring that all learners have sufficient opportunity to be included and actively involved in the learning process and that they are treated fairly, equally and their differences are recognised, accommodated and where relevant celebrated.
Initial assessment	Initial assessment is a formal and informal process that identifies each learner's starting point. It helps to identify learners' current levels of ability and their need for support and is often used to place learners at a particular level of study.
Internal verification	This is a centre devised quality assurance process which assures the assessment against the awarding organisation unit grading criteria (i.e. making sure that learners' responses meet the requirements of the unit assessment criteria) and that assignment briefs are fit for purpose (i.e. are capable of allowing learners to generate the evidence required to pass the unit).
Internal Verifier	This is a member of staff able to verify assessor decisions, and validate assignments. The Internal Verifier records findings, gives assessor feedback, and oversees remedial action
Learner contract	A basic learner contract will outline the expected conduct from a learner, such as attendance, punctuality, abiding by the organisations policies and procedures, etc.
Learning aims/outcomes	This is what the learner should know, understand or be able to do as a result of completing the unit.

Lesson plans	A lesson plan is a lecturer's guide to delivering a particular session, including session aims, objectives, assessment strategies, session content and timeframe, learning resources to be used and lecturer and learner activities.
Mapping of recognition of prior learning	This is a formal process often devised by the awarding organisation where the learning provider maps the learner's prior learning (certificated and/or experiential) against each learning aim/outcome and assessment criteria of a unit and then submits it to the awarding organisation for consideration. If successful, the learner does not have to complete those assessment criteria that have been recognised as having been achieved through prior learning.
Ofqual	The Office of Qualifications and Examinations Regulation (Ofqual) regulates qualifications, examinations and assessments in England and vocational qualifications in Northern Ireland. Ofqual is a non-ministerial department.
Pedagogy / pedagogical	These are the methods and practices in teaching, especially of children (up to the age of 18), where the focus is on the teacher's methods of transferring knowledge to a learner, who is dependent on the teacher's methods and understanding. The teacher controls the learning experience for children, and most teaching is based on a rigid curricula. A great deal of importance is placed on the grades achieved.
Peer assessment	Peer assessment involves learners taking responsibility for assessing the work of their peers against set assessment criteria.
Pre-assessment standardisation	Internal pre-assessment standardisation is a process within a centre / learning

	provider for checking an initial sample of internal assessments / marking / grading to ensure it is consistent across all assessors before assessors continue assessing / marking / grading. This process only applies to internally assessed learner work.
Qualification specification	awarding organisations publish qualification specifications for their centres / learning providers to use in developing and delivering the awarding organisation courses. The qualification specification sets out what is required of the learner in order to achieve the qualification, it contains information about permitted unit combinations and information specific to managing and delivering the qualification(s) including specific quality assurance requirements.
Reasonable adjustment	In the context of learning providers, a reasonable adjustment is an alteration that a learning provider makes to enable a disabled learner to continue to carry out their duties without being at a disadvantage compared to other learners.
Recognition of prior learning (RPL)	RPL recognises prior learning, whether the result of a formal course of study or learning through experience. RPL is the term used by awarding organisations and is equivalent to APL.
Safeguarding	Safeguarding is a term which is broader than 'child protection' and relates to the action taken to promote the welfare of children and protect them from harm. Safeguarding is defined in Working together to safeguard children 2013 as: <ul><li>protecting children from maltreatment</li><li>preventing impairment of children's health and development</li></ul>

	• ensuring that children grow up in circumstances consistent with the provision of safe and effective care and • taking action to enable all children to have the best outcomes
Schemes of work	A scheme of work is a guideline that defines the structure and content of a course. It maps out clearly how resources (e.g. books, equipment, time) and class activities (e.g. lecturing, group work, practicals, discussions) and assessment strategies (e.g. tests, assignments, homework) will be used to ensure that the learning outcomes and assessment criteria or assessment objectives of the course are met successfully. It will normally include times and dates. The scheme of work is usually an interpretation of a qualification specification and unit or module guides.
Self-assessment	Self-assessment requires learners to reflect on their own work and judge how well they have performed in relation to the assessment criteria.
Standardisation	Internal standardisation is a process within a centre / learning provider for checking that internal assessment / marking / grading is accurate and consistent across all assessors. This process only applies to internally assessed learner work.
Standards Verifier (SV)	This is an external verification process used to check centre assignments and assessment against national standards, and internal verification processes.
Unit guide	These outline the unit aims, learning outcomes, assessment criteria, unit content, grading criteria and provide some guidance.

Printed in Great Britain
by Amazon

16899333R00068